PROFITING FROM DIVERSITY

PROFITING FROM DIVERSITY

Trevor Bentley and Susan Clayton

Gower

Published by
Gower Publishing Limited
Gower House
Croft Road
Aldershot
Hampshire GU11 3HR
England

HF
5549
,B438
1998

Gower
Old Post Road
Brookfield
Vermont 05036
USA

British Library Cataloguing in Publication Data

Bentley, Trevor J.
    Profiting from diversity
    1. Diversity in the workplace
    I. Title   II. Clayton, Susan
    658.3'0089

ISBN 0 566 07931 3

Library of Congress Cataloging-in-Publication Data
Bentley, Trevor J.
    Profiting from diversity / by Trevor Bentley and Susan Clayton.
        p.   cm.
    Includes index.
    ISBN 0-566-07931-3 (hbk.)
    – 1. Diversity in the workplace.   I. Clayton, Susan, 1950–
    II. Title.
    HF5549.B438 1998   97-42339
    658.3'008—dc21   CIP

Typeset in Century Old Style by Raven Typesetters, Chester and printed in Great Britain by Biddles Limited, Guildford.

Contents

List of figures

'This perspective is intuitive, it makes good sense, but how can I begin to make it work in my organization?'

This book presents a different and challenging view of diversity in organizations and businesses, which is likely to raise many questions.

Trevor Bentley and Susan Clayton wish to encourage improved diversity practice and therefore invite you to ask questions and engage in discussions that could assist you in achieving this for yourself and in your organization.

You can e-mail them at:

etcoffice@compuserve.com

where Trevor and Susan will respond and attempt to answer questions that you raise. Although they do not promise an immediate turnaround as they also consult widely, they will endeavour to reply to all e-mails.

That one question asked could result in major changes for your organization and in your personal career.

THE COMPANY WAY

Once upon a time,
  As often happens in the world of business,
    A bright, creative young man earned a promotion.
      His new responsibilities and position
        Seemed stressful and a bit scary.
          Moving to the company's headquarters
            Was a big change for him and his family.

                    However, once he was established,
                      The bright young man discovered
                        That, even though his new office was larger
                          And his authority had broader limits,
                            His staff members were friendly
                              And his boss was supportive.
                                He was well pleased
                                  And he didn't feel as stressed or scared.

Then one day
  His boss said, 'We need to reduce costs.
    We think you are just the man
      To head up the project and meet the challenge.'
        The bright, creative young man was happy;
          He admired his boss and relished challenges.
            Anxious to get started,
              He entered his office and began to think.

                    He worked furiously for the rest of the day
                      And the next morning, too.
                        Then, as was his custom,
                          He placed his brainstormed ideas
                            On the back burner,
                                And he turned to more routine tasks.

Later that week, the boss came to the man's office
And he asked the man about the project.
'Well, how is it going? What do you have for me?'
The boss spoke with enthusiasm and anticipation.
Proudly the man shared his brainstorming ideas,
And mapped out his alternative solutions,
Saying he'd need more time to complete his work.

'Wait a minute,' his boss interrupted,
 'I didn't ask for maybes and could bes.
  We need answers – and now!'
   The man sat back in his chair, puzzled
    By his boss's angry tone.
     He admired his boss and wanted to please him.
      'You've got to learn to solve problems
       Like our other managers do.
        That has been our road to success.
         Try again and do it right this time.'

        The boss left shaking his head
       And the man put his rejected ideas in the bin.
      Soon after this the man visited his daughter's school
     As the loving father of a young girl.
    He was proud to see a painting his daughter had done.
   It was a flower in bloom.
  And it stood out from the others on display.

                    As he observed the class
                    He overheard the teacher say,
                    'You will need to change your flower.
                    It has a blue not a green stem,
                    And it's not like the others.
                    The petals should be yellow.'
                    The young girl liked her teacher
                    And she wanted to please her.
                    Her father watched her take her
                    Flower off the wall.

Later that evening at home,
    The man spoke with his daughter.
'I like your flower, but it wasn't acceptable.
    You will need to do it the teacher's way,
That will be your road to success.'
    His daughter sat silently and listened.
She loved and respected her dad.
    'Try again, love, but do it right this time,' he said.

After supper she took her picture of a flower
And hung it in her bedroom.
Then she sat down and painted another flower.
This time the flower had a green stem,
And yellow petals.
She worked hard to make it look like all the others.

    The next morning at work the man
    Was asked by his boss to attend a workshop.
    His boss told him that this would help
    To lead him to the company way of doing things.
    The man liked to try new approaches.
    He enjoyed learning new things.
    So he entered the workshop positively.

The programme was fixed in black and white.
    The leader said it would be followed.
    No additions or changes were allowed.
    The man wanted to learn.
    He admired and respected his peers.
    Some of the ideas he liked,
    Others he disagreed with.
    He explored colourful alternatives,
    And asked 'what ifs'.

    Each time he tried to do this,
    A fellow member of the group would help him.
    'We don't do things that way here,
    We deal in black and white,
    It's our tried and tested road to success.
That is the company way.'

At first the man asked more questions.
He tried to find out why and to explore the spectrum of ideas.
But then each member's response left a mark.
He was learning the company way.
He was a creative, bright man
Though he still liked some of his colourful ideas best.

That night the man helped his daughter.
She had to review a book and she had brought home the teacher's rules.
Together they worked on the review.
The daughter loved her father
And she liked to try new things.
'Can't I paint a picture of the characters?'
The girl enjoyed using her paints.
'No. These rules say to use ink only.'
The man helped his daughter.

    'Why can't I tell them what I hate about the book?'
    'Because, love, it says to tell why you liked it.'
    'Can't I use the computer to print it?'
    'It says hand-written here,' her dad replied.
    Carefully they reviewed all the rules.
    The girl worked hard to follow them.

    At last the review was finished.
    The girl didn't like it much.
    She thought it dull.
    But her father liked it,
    And she wanted to please her dad.

In the week that followed,
 The man toiled over his project work.
  He spent countless hours writing and rewriting,
   Keeping in mind all the time
    The advice of his peers from the workshop.
     Once in a while he found himself slipping
      Into the old habits of questioning,
       Trying to explore the kaleidoscope of ideas that filled his head.
      But, being well-disciplined,
       He repressed these urges.

He pressed for the untainted truth.
As a final check
He sent his proposal
To some of his peers.
It returned with many comments.
'It's too radical.'
'Don't try this.'
'This is good, it's worked before.'
'You've almost got it!'
'It's logical, black and white.'

He revised the proposal accordingly
And at last he was done.
He didn't really like it.
It was long-winded and stale.
His work was usually like
A fresh breeze in a woodland in the spring.
This was more like a dark forest in winter.
He submitted his proposal a day early.
He wanted to please his boss.

Driving home from work
The man thought about his new position.
He felt comfortable now.
He had more confidence in himself.
Silently he admitted that his peers
In their wisdom had helped him.
It had been much easier to do this project,
Much easier than any before.
He didn't feel at all stressed.
He felt comfortably calm and quiet.
He was certain he was on the road to success.

There was, of course, no thrill, or electric excitement.
The vibrancy and colour of his work was missing
But, then, so was the strain.
The 'company way' felt more comfortable, safer.

He picked up his daughter from netball practice
And asked her about the book review.
'I got an A,' she said.
'Great! See how well you did?'
The father gave his daughter a hug.
'How do you feel now about the teacher's way?'
The girl sat quietly for a moment.
'OK, I think I really don't feel anything about it.'
'That's how it should be, you know,'
The father explained gently. 'It's more comfortable that way.'

> The next morning
> The boss called the man into his office.
> 'Sit down, sit down. We need to talk.
> I've reviewed your proposal.
> I want to congratulate you!
> You've found it – the "company way".
> You're on the road to success.'
> And the boss shook the man's hand.

> 'Now we have another project for you,
> But we want you to be creative with it.
> You handled the last project so well.
> Have fun on the road to success.'
> And he heard the details about his new project.
> He took many notes, but he asked no questions.
> He left the office calmly that evening.
> He didn't feel excited, he felt nothing.
> The new project wasn't really a challenge.
> He didn't need to start work on it yet,
> After all, he knew the company way now.

When he got home
He went to see his daughter in her room.
He noticed the painting of a flower on her desk.
He walked over and smiled a proud smile.
His daughter had learned to paint a flower.
She had painted it the teacher's way.
She was on the road to success.
The flower was perfect.
The stem was green.
Its petals yellow.
Just the same as all the rest.

By Elaine Biech
*The ASTD Trainer's Sourcebook: Creativity
and Innovation*, McGraw-Hill, NY

1 Strategic diversity

INTRODUCTION

New strategic paradigms are needed if we are to embrace diversity fully and sustain the fundamental change that is now called for. This means that we must address the behaviours and the underlying forces that are indicative of conforming cultures and which are also typical of most organizations. Change means that a business can become more diverse in the marketplace as well as more diverse internally – that is, in bringing out the rich diversity of the workforce and realizing the potential that people bring to work with them.

DIVERSITY AND UNITY

The new paradigm that we propose is one that balances diversity and conformity in a way that leads to unity (Figure 1.1). Unity comes about through people connecting with each other in their differences, in other words valuing and respecting difference. People feel fulfilled through the appropriate release of their full potential in their work, and feel that they belong because of the respect and recognition they receive from others, for their uniqueness. Belonging needs are fundamental to human existence but become misplaced in over-conforming cultures where people's uniqueness is dulled. The model that we offer here is a balanced way of working together, one that enriches the business *and* provides for people's belonging needs.

In the new paradigm diversity pervades every corner of the organization, every level that exists in the organization, every contact that is made outside the organization: from finance to personnel; from production to sales; from marketing to customer service, and so on. No one is excluded. People think differently, act differently towards each other and bring a different energy into their work. We are all in this together, from top executives, to bottom-line workers, to external consultants. The only boundary that diversity has is in its 'appropriateness', which we call

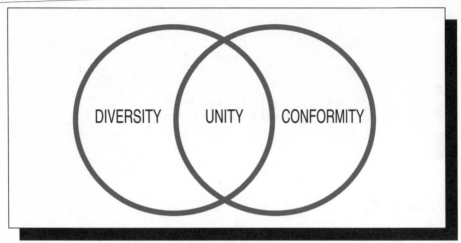

Figure 1.1 Balancing diversity and conformity

'appropriate diversity'. It comes about through the tension between diversity and conformity, and is managed at its best when unity is attained.

WHY IS UNITY SO IMPORTANT?

Unity is an outcome of diversity practice, not an input. Unity is people coming together collectively through valuing difference. Unity is what we seek to achieve by bringing into balance diversity and conformity. Through unity we find that we are recognized and appreciated for the uniqueness that we bring to the situation: we belong because of our individuality, as well as our commonalities. Until now most organizations have expected employees to 'fit in' with the culture, which would have been fine had that also meant 'fitting in *and* standing out'. Over the years, however, 'fitting in' has come to mean leaving your unique self at the entrance to the workplace and bringing your 'same as everyone else' self inside.

Conformity is about connecting with others through 'giving up' difference; unity is connecting with others through valuing difference. If there is no valuing of difference real unity does not occur. In order to unite we have to experience, know and understand the differences that exist around us. Unity is a healthy, productive process that can provide a suitable environment in which we can fulfil our human needs for belonging.

In the new paradigm 'fitting in' means being appropriately diverse. This entails being not so diverse that you create anarchy, but bringing your unique self to achieve your potential in your work and to contribute to the potential of the business. People bring a wonderful richness into organizations, a tapestry of colour that can offer novelty, innovation, curiosity, unpredictability, unusual connections

– a whole range of possibilities. Such qualities exist because people exist. Profiting from diversity means bringing this richness into the workplace.

DIVERSITY AND CHANGE

Diversity does not have a beginning or an end – it is continuously evolving and changing. The first task is to commit to the journey: in other words, organizations should become travelling companions with other organizations in this world of diversity.

Diversity already exists in every organization, so 'change' is about changing the current path to find a route that will allow the richness of diversity to emerge:

The current path	*The new route*
Deterministic	Emergent
Capability makes a difference	Adaptability makes a difference
Task focused	People focused
Systems oriented	Relationship oriented
Doing a job	Releasing potential
Putting in	Drawing out
People are their roles	People are people who also have roles
Valuing similarities	Valuing difference
Seeing things from *few* perspectives	Seeing things from *many* perspectives
Working with limitations	Working with choice
Confusion about diversity	Clarity with diversity

The predicament we are currently in – the predicament of conformity – arises simply because the path we are on is going in the wrong direction. Changing to a new route does not mean having to throw out old ways of working. The new paradigm means finding a different route that brings old ways of working into balance with new thinking and practice. This will require letting go of some old beliefs and mindsets. But we should not leap from one predicament to another by throwing the baby out with the bathwater. For instance, the new route is not about throwing away *capability* for the sake of *adaptability,* or weakening the *task focus* for the sake of *people focus.* In diversity all of these aspects have a place of value.

DISCOVERING STRATEGIC DIVERSITY

Operating strategically with diversity means integrating two very different ways of

3

working. In her book *Sharpen Your Team's Skills in Developing Strategy* (1997) Susan Clayton explains how strategists today need to think in terms of both determined and emergent processes to achieve the best possible outcomes in their business:

> **Determined strategy** is the development of logical and intentional steps towards achieving a specific outcome.
>
> Strategy formation is the process of developing plans, schemes and procedures to establish direction for action and achieve a predetermined outcome. These plans hold a strong quantitative, analytical function based on shared vision and shared ideologies. There exists a sequential process which provides a logical order with logical steps towards achieving an outcome.
>
> **Emergent strategy** is building on the converging of new and often diverse ideas for the fulfilment of purpose.
>
> Today strategic management increasingly includes a practice of understanding patterns and shapes of the business; connecting past patterns and future expectations with emerging patterns in the everyday flow of events. Strategy formation takes on new shapes.
>
> This is not to say that past practices are being thrown out; on the contrary, the linear approach, which in itself has a pattern, still plays a part in strategic thinking. The essence is that different, non-linear patterns now play an important role in developing strategy. These patterns can be understood in emerging processes. This process requires people to be open, flexible and willing to learn. The ideas of different people in an organization converge over time. Strategies grow out of collective action. (Clayton 1997, pp. 16–18)

With strategic diversity we are *tapping into* something that already exists, so we need to build on emergent processes. These are processes that release the wide array of potential that exists on a moment-by-moment basis, in contrast to looking for results in the future through predetermined capabilities. It is a process of *drawing out* rather than *putting in* (Figure 1.2).

Most of us are well practised in deterministic ways of working, and we know the benefits and the limitations of these. Many of us have also been practising emergent approaches for many years, but because traditionally such practice has not been valued as a strategic business style the result is a process of wrapping up emergent processes in deterministic language. For instance, many people respond intuitively to situations, then in hindsight speak of them in a predetermined way – like the chef who burnt the dinner rolls and intuitively mixed together a last-minute substitute, which went down so well that it eventually became a speciality. He took credit for his recipe but talked about it to his boss as though it had been intentional.

Emergent processes are essential skills to be valued and developed in order to travel on the diversity route, because:

4

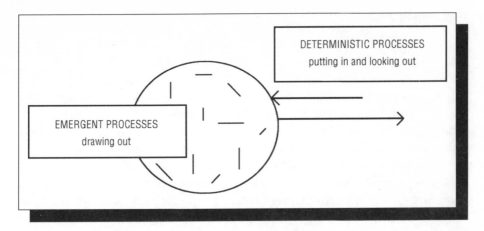

Figure 1.2 Processes of determined and emergent strategy

1 Diversity already exists within the organization: therefore it isn't something out there to be brought in, or something that will happen sometime in the future.
2 Diversity is about people and human systems, which require a different frame of reference from technical or operational systems.
3 Diversity cannot be predetermined: we do not know the quality and content of the diversity that exists until we tap into it.

We will not even begin to discover the extent of the diversity that exists in organizations until we bring determined and emergent processes into balance. We still need our visions, strategies and planning processes, but the richness of diversity emerges in the workplace in daily, even momentary occurrences. Determinism encourages people to focus on the future. When people concentrate only on the future the moment-by-moment richness is not seen: it arises and then dissipates. Emergent strategies are critical in making important connections, and it is in these moment-by-moment occurrences that diversity comes into being.

A FRAMEWORK FOR DIVERSITY

Because this new paradigm affects everyone in the organization the focus of change shifts from a deterministic focus on policies, procedures and legislation to an emergent focus:

● focus on people;
● focus on relationships;
● focus on performance;
● focus on 'appropriate diversity'.

5

FOCUS ON PEOPLE

Organizational culture is the collective behaviours of all the people that work in that organization. People co-create the culture in which they work. Culture change is frequently talked about as though it is shaped through intent, like landscaping a garden. The truth is that the culture is continually being re-created, day in, day out, through the interactions and collective personalities of the people in the organization, even though it appears to stay pretty much the same most of the time. This sense of stability occurs because people follow set norms. When a culture needs shifting these norms need to be challenged.

Diversity is hidden in a culture by the requirements to *perform* and the demands to *conform*. In organizations that demand conformity diversity remains hidden and will only appear when people are willing to shift. And it is only when people are willing to shift that change will happen.

Diversity calls for an environment that is open enough, honest enough and trusting enough for people to bring their true selves into the workplace; a safe enough environment where people can challenge attitudes, fears and established patterns of behaviour that in the past have inhibited potential.

The notion of 'enough' is very important. Anxieties can arise when expectations are not clarified and differences not respected. What is perceived as open and honest to one person may be very different to another. 'Enough' is a boundary defined by people interacting with each other, through testing out and through respect.

Focusing on people is essential to thinking strategically about diversity:

- People co-create the culture and the environment in which they work.
- People co-create the relationships between the business and external bodies.
- People co-create the relationships within the organization.
- People co-create and innovate new products and services.
- People co-create and manage the systems for running the business.
- People co-create the vision and direction of the business.
- People co-create the strategies, policies and procedures for the organization.
- People co-create strategic diversity.

People bring a rich wealth of diversity into your organization – and that includes you. In turn it is only you and these same people who can enable diversity to become visible. To do this you need to encourage learning, offer the right support for people to take risks and seek to release individual and collective potential in the organization.

FOCUS ON RELATIONSHIPS

Diversity and unity are an outcome of good relationships, so a focus on relationships is critical to strategic diversity. That means refining *interpersonal* and *group* skills.

Interpersonal skills

This means going beyond the interpersonal teachings that many people experience in their working lives, such as listening, mirroring and good questioning techniques. New interpersonal skills require people to engage in 'quality contact' in their interactions with others. This quality contact means understanding the blocks that interfere with interpersonal contact, for example making assumptions about the other person and acting as though they are true, without checking them out.

Quality contact also includes effective challenge and productive conflict management. Conflicting views are a quality of diversity, and good conflict management enables productive outcomes. Conflict management skills are weakened in conforming cultures because challenge and conflict are reduced to a minimum and so there is little opportunity to learn.

Through quality contact a dramatic shift takes place in the way people engage with each other. The following list illustrates the difference between interpersonal interactions in conforming cultures and good contact in diverse cultures:

From conformity ⟶ *To diversity*

From conformity	To diversity
Shallow conversation	Engaging dialogue
Prejudging	Reserving judgement
Denying your prejudices	Owning your prejudices
Focusing on commonalities	Valuing uniqueness
Jealousy	Curiosity
Conflict denial or avoidance	Conflict management
Blame	Learning together
Seeking similarity	Seeking novelty
Avoiding difference	Seeking difference
Closed and defensive	Open and receptive
Self-protecting	Caring of self and others
Denying your uniqueness	Wearing your uniqueness with pride
Deference to a few	All people have something of value to offer
Denying personal fears	Acknowledging personal fears
Withholding assumptions	Challenging and checking out assumptions

7

Group skills

The focus on relationships in groups is twofold: 1) the way the leader leads the group, 2) the way people behave in the group. Strategic diversity means that both the leader and the group members take responsibility for balancing diversity and conformity within the group.

Diversity stands out more in groups than on an interpersonal level, simply because there is more of it. In a group of six people one member has five others to compare with, in contrast to one other at an interpersonal level. Social pressure to conform rather than stand out can deny the group its diversity.

Through strategic diversity group leaders and group members discover the art, and the benefits, of diversity, enabling the diversity within the group to be released into the work of the group.

FOCUS ON PERFORMANCE

When we consider performance in a culture of diversity we must shift our thinking into a new paradigm. We must begin to widen the scope of performance and understand the range of influences that impact on performance collectively and individually. The key points to address are:

- releasing individual and collective potential through recognizing difference;
- recognizing the scope of *what* people are able to do;
- recognizing that people differ in *how* they do what they do.

In an organization where strategic diversity is regarded as critical to the way people work together, performance increases through surfacing and releasing the full potential that people bring to the workplace, individually and collectively. This is true for top management right through to the bottom line. It does not necessarily mean that people *do more* of what they are already doing. In fact it might mean that they do less of what they are currently doing in order to bring into the workplace more of themselves in a different way. This means that the focus is as much on *how* people do what they do, as on *what* they can do.

For instance:

A manager noticed that some people in the department seemed to be more energetic first thing in the morning than others, so she decided to find out more. In her enquiries she discovered that people work at different speeds and differ in their performance depending on the time of day. As an experiment she decided to offer flexible working hours, with employees jointly taking the responsibility for setting and keeping track of the hours that they worked.

Of course the experiment made a beneficial difference to productivity. Performance increased, not just because the new pattern drew on the best of people's 'energy time', but also because people had choice as well as their differences being respected and valued.

This example focused on *how* people do their work. Changing the *how* impacted on the *what* – in this case, positively.

Something that happens when organizations begin to engage with diversity in the new paradigm is that they discover the importance of *choice*. Lack of choice narrows difference; increasing choice is a clear recognition of difference. Giving employees the responsibility of managing the boundaries around choicefulness adds to the trust that supports a healthy culture where diversity is practised.

FOCUS ON 'APPROPRIATE DIVERSITY'

A concern that many people raise when discussing diversity in this new paradigm is that it can lead to anarchy, that people will have too much freedom in their self-expression, which in turn will lead to a breakdown of the system. This is true, just as it is also true that conformity to the extreme will also break down systems. Many organizations are sitting unwittingly on the edge of breaking down through over-conformity. There is a need to recognize what is appropriate and what is not for each unique system. Discovering what is 'appropriate diversity' is critical to the new diversity paradigm.

Appropriate diversity reflects a tension between conformity and diversity – that is, the extent to which people can 'tolerate' conforming to certain norms within the system, and the extent to which the system can 'tolerate' the expression of individual difference. The minimum requirement in a system will be for people to

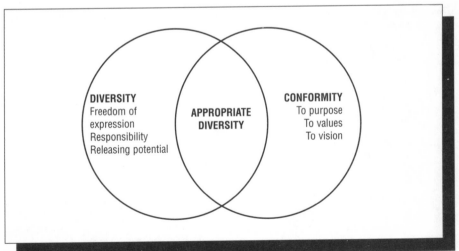

Figure 1.3 'Appropriate diversity'

conform to the vision, the purpose and the values of that system. In return the system will need to enable freedom of expression, responsibility and the release of potential (Figure 1.3).

Developing an ability to discriminate between what is appropriate and what is not means experimenting and taking risks. Discovering difference, what is appropriate and what is not, is a continuous learning process. To support this learning process people need to think and act in a different way from the patterns that prevail in conforming environments.

CONCLUSION

The new paradigm of strategic diversity focuses on the richness that already exists in an organization. To fully realize the potential of an organization emergent processes are needed – processes and skills which release the diversity and the potential of the workforce. Strategic diversity means that people throughout the organization pay attention to the way that they think and act towards each other and thus are encouraged to find the balance between conformity and diversity, to achieve unity. Thinking strategically about diversity is necessary to enable diversity to be released. Strategic diversity is the challenge that we are faced with in this new paradigm, and this is what we address in the rest of the book.

REFERENCE

Clayton, Susan (1997) *Sharpen Your Team's Skills in Developing Strategy*, London: McGraw-Hill.

2 Bottom-line benefits

INTRODUCTION

The bottom line, whether it is measured by profits earned, improved shareholder value or increased share price, is the *raison d'être* of all businesses. Without the added value and hence surplus that businesses generate they could not exist. There would be no value for customers, employees and shareholders to share.

Paradoxically bottom-line benefits are not produced by 'bottom-line thinking'. They are the result of visionary zeal supported by excellent strategic thinking. Or, if you prefer, bottom-line benefits come from top-line thinking.

Bottom-line benefits are produced when 'income streams' exceed 'cost streams', in other words when more flows in than flows out. This simple perspective, true but frequently misunderstood, can and has led to the widespread, erroneous and highly destructive practice of 'downsizing'.

Downsizing does not work because the simple perspective of income flowing in and cost flowing out has not been recognized as a cyclical dependent process. In other words cost streams actually generate income streams and vice versa. Unlike the chicken and the egg story we know which comes first, and that is the cost stream. However, in order to explain the impact diversity has we shall start by looking at income streams – just to be 'different', as it were.

INCOME STREAMS

Income streams are generated by creativity and innovation linked to a high degree of adaptability and responsiveness to the marketplace. Diversity is important in all aspects of developing, managing and maintaining income streams and is particularly noticeable in three ways.

11

MARKET DIFFERENTIATION

For a long time salespeople have realized how vital it is to be able to differentiate the product or service they sell from their competitors' products. Good salespeople know that even when they have done a good job of identifying their customers' needs and have reacted well to their buying signals they still need to be able to offer that 'unique selling point', or preferably several, that sets their product or service apart from the competition.

When such unique selling points become significant and valued differentiations it is possible to charge a premium price and so increase income streams and margins. Looking for, valuing and highlighting diversity in products and services leads directly to bottom-line benefits.

Of course for this to work the 'uniqueness' inherent in differentiation has to add to the product's effectiveness, quality, appearance and appeal to customers. It has, in other words, to be 'appropriate diversity'.

CUSTOMER LOYALTY

Income streams have to be maintained and increased by encouraging customers to keep buying and talking favourably about the products and services you provide. This can be done in many ways, from financial inducements, discounts, and so on to offering special facilities for regular customers.

Air miles for travellers and loyalty cards with increased offers when you reach higher and higher levels of business are modern examples of innovation and diversity in maintaining customer loyalty.

Being different in treating customers so that they want to remain customers is not new. However, the quality of products and services has improved so much that it is increasingly difficult to differentiate between different suppliers. This problem is something which has given added impetus to the 'customer service' philosophy and there is no doubt that businesses that are able to approach customers in an attractive, satisfying and diverse way will earn their continuing support.

PRODUCT LIFE-CYCLES

All products and services have life-cycles, running from the original birth of the product through to its eventual death. Some life-cycles are measured in days (newspapers), some in months (computer technology) and others in years (confectionery). Whatever the life-cycle might be it is important that as products die new ones are ready to replace the old. This process has increased rapidly in recent years as product life-cycles have shortened and competition has become fiercer.

Diversity in research and development is crucial, not only in the design process but also in reacting differently to influence the market rather than to follow competitors. The Dyson vacuum cleaner is a perfect example of this. Rather than develop a similar but better product than the competition James Dyson set out to produce a completely different product, which is now the best-selling vacuum cleaner in the world. After many efforts (over 5000 prototypes) Dyson perfected his cyclonic system, dispensing with bags and improving cleaning performance. The machine, selling at a premium price, looks good and is easier to use, more robust, and more colourful than the competition.

Proactive adaptation and response to market interest is diversity at its very best – being different not for the sake of it, but to add value and appeal. The Dyson vacuum cleaner is a prime example of diversity at work.

COST STREAMS

There are two types of cost stream:

- those that directly generate income streams, which we can call 'product costs' ('product' as used in this context can also mean a service);
- those that do not directly generate income streams, but which are necessary for managing the business, which we can call 'management costs'.

Product costs are all those cost streams which purchase the materials, facilities and people skills necessary to produce and market the product or service that the customer buys. Product cost streams would include the vital costs of training and development and quality management that lead to improved products and services. Any way in which these cost streams can be reduced which improves income streams is what we call 'productivity'.

Management costs are those costs of providing the facilities and the support services for the business. This might include offices, information systems, management teams, top management, and so on. These are the costs of providing the visionary zeal and the strategic thinking so essential to successful business. Any way in which these management cost streams can be reduced without affecting the quality of management is what we call 'efficiency'.

DIVERSITY AND PRODUCTIVITY

It is possible to achieve productivity gains by doing the same things faster and better, but these gains are relatively insignificant. What improves productivity more than anything else is diversity – doing things differently.

For many years people working in the area of productivity have known about the importance of doing things differently. They know about looking for changes in working practices, changes in materials that are used, changes in design and changes in thinking about products and services – in other words the highest possible application of diversity thinking through creativity and innovation.

In searching for productivity improvements the exhortation has always been: 'How can we do things differently?' In today's fast-moving world of international markets this is perhaps even more important than it has ever been.

DIVERSITY AND EFFICIENCY

There are many organizations where the management cost streams are completely out of any realistic proportion to income streams. When management costs start to consume the gains made through productivity improvement, there is clearly something wrong.

Management costs are necessary but should be kept to the absolute minimum. There is one simple question that can be asked to determine the value of any management cost stream: 'If this management cost stream was eliminated or reduced would it damage the long-term success of the business?' The 'long-term' nature of the damage is crucial here because there are many reductions that could be made that would not damage the short-term success of the business. In fact, such reductions might even improve the bottom line in the short term. This is why downsizing often leads to the destruction of the business, because of the short-term nature of the savings and the long-term fatal damage that such savings can cause.

So diversity in finding ways to be more efficient should focus on finding different and less costly ways to manage, through operating less top-heavy management structures and through simplifying the rules and procedures for managing the business. Organizations which operate diversity in management cost streams are those which:

- value and reward creativity;
- reward risk-taking even when it does not prove successful;
- operate a policy of open management and encourage people to say what they think;
- encourage people to be passionate about what they do and allow them to do the things they feel passionate about;
- treat mistakes as opportunities to learn;
- push boundaries to the limits;
- trust people;
- operate a policy of freedom with responsibility.

In other words highly efficient organizations with low management cost streams operate differently and encourage their people to be different in their attitudes and approach to managing the business.

DIVERSITY AND QUALITY

Diversity is about *beating* standards and not about meeting standards.

Diversity is constrained when people are given standards that they have to meet. Individual performance is constrained when people are given standards to meet. Yet standards are important.

Standards are the minimum that people should be expected to beat in every way possible. This usually means doing things differently. Here is an example:

In one bank people are allocated to different duties each day – administration, foreign exchange, front counter, and so on. When queues form at the counters the staff allocated to counter duty have to try to cope and the quality of service declines.

In another bank people are allocated primary duties and are expected to move to wherever they see a need during the day. In this bank as queues form at the counter staff move from what they are doing to working at the counter and the quality of service is maintained at a high level.

In this example the second bank have different operating standards and expect staff to have the training to react and be able to do things differently in response to a perceived need. Consequently staff need diverse skills and the freedom to choose to change what they are doing when they deem it is necessary.

PERSONAL PERFORMANCE AND DIVERSITY

Individuals perform better when they are involved in planning what is expected of them, when they are trusted to be self-managing and when they are free to respond in the best way they can to what is happening.

To support and encourage high performance, management need to offer freedom and choice to people about what they do and how they do it. This freedom needs to be linked with the responsibility people have for quality work and for beating their performance plans. Of course the degree and levels of responsibility will normally be bounded by essential checks and controls which should be minimized.

Managers should encourage people to be different and to work differently rather than to fit in with some norm that management perceive to be appropriate. This is hard for many managers to achieve because they see people doing things differently from how they might do it themselves. Yet this degree of diversity is exactly what enables people to tap into their potential and to perform at higher than expected levels and consequently increase income streams and reduce cost streams.

PUSHING BOUNDARIES

Embracing diversity is not about looking for and finding a 'right way' of organizing and managing the business. It is about constantly questioning what is being done and the ways things are done and looking for different things to do and different ways to do things.

Diversity is about being different not once but all the time. So the new way, which is different from the old way, will itself soon become the old way and will need to be questioned.

Diversity is not about making change happen – it will happen anyway. Diversity is about accepting change and being different all the time.

But what of continuity and stability? What about a time of quiet and calm?

Continuity and stability are in no way inconsistent with diversity. In fact it is through the search for unity – the balance between conformity and diversity – that continuity and sustainability are possible. It is through being different and adaptable and welcoming change that continuity is assured. And, paradoxically, it is by constantly adjusting and adapting to the winds of change that the organizational ship can maintain its stability.

It is when we fight to stay the same, when we do not bend in the breeze, that the wind of change can wreak so much havoc. The quiet and calm that follows every storm is only a lull before the next storm. We create our own quiet and calm in organizations by learning how to handle change and by constantly being different in how we react and respond to what is happening.

When people focus on 'this is how it is' rather than on 'this is how it should be', then they are able to respond more realistically. Plans are intended to help people deal effectively with the future, not to make the future fit the plan. It is interesting to note that when organizations take this approach to diversity 'how it is' is nearly always substantially better than 'how it should have been'.

CONCLUSION

Diversity improves the bottom line through maintaining and improving income streams and through improving productivity and efficiency by focusing on cost streams. People perform better and beat standards and plans by being allowed the freedom to be diverse in what they do and how they do it. By embracing diversity change becomes an ally rather than an enemy. By being different and constantly adjusting and adapting to what is happening continuity and stability are assured. It is when we battle to keep the *status quo* that the organization's survival is threatened.

3 Working with diversity

INTRODUCTION

If bottom-line benefits come from top-line thinking then surely it follows that the people working in the organization need to conform with top-line thinking? The answer is both yes and no.

Yes, people *do* need to accept and take some ownership of the vision and the strategic thinking that emanates from the top. But no, people should *not* be expected to conform to the limited ideas of how the vision can be achieved that may emanate from the top except in so far as it provides the unity so essential for success.

CONFORMITY AND DIVERSITY – A DYNAMIC BALANCE

What is needed is a dynamic balance between conformity and diversity – that is, unity – with every demand to conform being questioned and a choice made, either intuitively or rationally, to conform or not. When this happens there is a dynamic interplay between conformity and diversity, and the balance only emerges if conformity is challenged. And most people only challenge conformity when they are encouraged to be diverse.

So, paradoxically, valuable and effective conformity only occurs when diversity is valued and encouraged. When people conform without making a choice about what they are doing then the conformity is unhealthy and individual diversity and potential are diminished.

In the film *The Dead Poets' Society* Robin Williams played the role of a teacher who was encouraging his students to embrace their diversity and question conformity. He naturally came up against the desire of the school principal for conformity and deference to 'how we do things here'. One student who was not allowed by his father to choose the career he wanted killed himself. The progressive teacher was blamed for 'putting such dangerous ideas into his students' heads'. Unfortunately this is a common scenario in many organizations where failure to conform with the organization's way of doing things can lead to a lack of advancement or dismissal. In these organizations the best approach is to 'keep your head down' and not to take any risks.

WE ARE ALL MIRACLES

Individual uniqueness is unquestionable. We are all natural and unique miracles. If you stop for a moment to think about yourself as a self-maintaining, organismically self-regulating, self-healing natural mechanism you should be amazed at what you are capable of. Nothing humankind has ever produced can even remotely replicate what we are able to achieve. Not even the total of all the computer power in the world can match the power of a single human brain.

It is unrealistic for anyone to expect individuals who are each so unique to want or need the same thing at the same time. Yet for all our differences we all, or most of us, have some need to belong, to be part of something where we are valued and loved. The family is the place where, for most people, this need is initially met and then as we grow we look for this belonging at school, in peer groups and at work. In other words we search for unity.

One way to belong that we learn very early in our development is to conform to the accepted behaviour of the group to which we want to belong. As our acceptance and sense of belonging becomes secure we can start to question the extent to which we want to conform. At this point we might be willing to risk being rejected by the group by refusing to conform. This risk might be rewarded with some adjustment of group expectations, but it could also be rewarded by rejection and the accompanying feelings of isolation. Testing what is possible and what is not acceptable is how we try to achieve the dynamic balance. Some of us have learned that life is safer and more secure if we lean towards a conforming pattern of behaviour, whilst others have discovered and enjoy the excitement and risk of differentiating ourselves at every possible opportunity. Of course differentiation means that life can often be very uncomfortable and lonely.

FITTING IN BY BEING DIFFERENT

It is possible but risky to 'fit in' by being different. This can happen if there is enough acceptance of group needs and yet a healthy level of questioning which does not threaten the group's existence. This is a difficult balance to establish and means that people need to swing from conformity to diversity and back again until they find a balance that they and the group are comfortable with.

This balance can only happen if people are encouraged to display their differences and to take risks in how they relate to others in the group. In organizations the degree of discomfort that this might cause often leads to a general acceptance of existing patterns of behaviour and an unhealthy level of conformity.

Conformity becomes unhealthy when organizations are perceived not to welcome any questioning of the current patterns of behaviour. It is unhealthy because it means that people will not take the risk of being different and this means that they will leave much of their potential behind them when they enter the organization. Imagine a sign at the entrance to an organization which reads:

> As you enter please leave at the desk your individuality, your creativity and your potential to be great. They are not welcome and you will not need them here.

Of course no organization of which the authors know displays such a sign, but many operate as if such a sign existed and this limits and constrains people to such an extent that performance is seriously hampered. When people are allowed/ encouraged to be different and to question patterns of behaviour they can bring their full capabilities into play.

DIVERSITY AT THE GROWING EDGE

One of the fascinating aspects of working with diversity is that when people explore and extend themselves they always do so at the limits of their individuality.

Figure 3.1   We are each unique

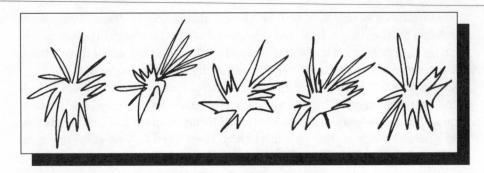

Figure 3.2 Unique human attributes

We will give a simple representation of this idea in the shape of a spiky blob (Figure 3.1).

At the centre of the blob are those human attributes that make us similar to other human beings. These are our basic attributes that group us in a general way, for example, men, women, Europeans, Asians, orientals, Africans, and so on. These attributes are not things we have chosen. We are born with them and they are usually those which are most apparent to others.

As we develop our individuality, personality and abilities our spikes grow until we become completely unique in shape. Much of this development has to do with how we learn to survive and grow in the environment in which we find ourselves. Some of us are much spikier than others and these differences in spikiness indicate how different we are, or have chosen to be (Figure 3.2).

CHOOSING TO BE DIFFERENT

The authors believe that diversity has a great deal to do with making choices. Of course it can be argued that many of our basic attributes are not chosen by us and that we have little choice about the environment in which we start life and grow and develop. However, what we do with who we are and how we choose to conform and/or differentiate is primarily a matter of personal choice.

There have been millions of moments in all our lives when we have made choices, and we continue to do so every day. The choices we make affect how we behave, how we learn and how we grow and develop our individuality. So as we make choices our spikes grow and we become different.

When we choose to conform we can do so while being aware of the reasons for making the choice. For example, you might not agree with some particular pattern of behaviour, but you conform because you do not want to offend or alienate others. Here is an example:

A manager was very much against the 'them and us' attitude that prevailed at his company between management and staff. He pointed out the ludicrous behaviour of managers eating behind a curtain drawn across part of the staff canteen. However, when he was promoted he started eating with the managers behind the curtain. When he was challenged about this he said, 'It would be churlish to make a big issue of it. Give me time and I will convince my colleagues to get rid of the curtain and to join the staff in the canteen.' Which in due course he did.

In this example the manager had deliberately chosen to conform so that later, when he had been accepted in the group, he could suggest some changes to how they behaved. This is working with unity.

Unfortunately many people do not have this level of awareness and simply 'go along' with the established pattern without questioning it or making a personal choice. The 'this is how we do things here' message is too strong.

PREFERENCES AND PREJUDICES

We all have preferences and prejudices. Our preferences have a lot to do with the choices we have made, the opportunities we have had and the many messages that we have received from parents, teachers, our peers and the media.

Prejudices are not about choice, they are conditioned or learned responses to particular situations, things and/or groups of individuals. Our prejudices have grown because we have not questioned these conditioned behaviours and so they have become embedded in who we are and influence how we behave.

If you think about the spiky diagram shown in Figure 3.1, you can think of prejudices as being at the core of your being, deeply ingrained in you. Similarly you can see your preferences as choices you make that develop your spikes and your individuality, as shown in Figure 3.2. We can go further than this and say that prejudices are unaware, unhealthy ways to respond, and preferences are healthy ways to respond to the world around us.

So we have a number of possibilities of reacting in healthy and unhealthy ways:

Healthy	*Unhealthy*
Choiceful conformity	Unquestioned compliance
Preferences	Prejudices
Choiceful differentiation	Differing for the sake of it
Open minded	Closed minded
Becoming spiky	Being frightened of our own and others' spikes
Accepting difference	Demanding conformity

BEING DIFFERENT

Like it or not you are different from every other human being who is living, has lived, or will ever live. You do not have to be different, you *are* different, just as the rest of us are. Yet what a lot of trouble we take to try to hide our differences. Here are just a few means of doing this:

- Hairstyles
- Clothes
- School uniforms
- Corporate wardrobes
- Common languages
- Rituals
- Sports
- Musical tastes.

In all these ways people hide their differences by wanting to be the same, to belong to this group or that group. Punks, mods, gothics, rockers, smart suits, fashionable, and so on are all examples of the need to identify with a group, to find others who are the same as us where we can choose to belong and to declare our belonging.

We cannot ignore something which appears to be a basic human need and drive. But neither do we have to enshrine this basic need in organizational behaviour by pandering to it. We can demand diversity just as we can demand conformity, but then diversity becomes just another way of conforming to the organizational pattern. 'Everybody is diverse here.'

Perhaps, and this suggestion is risky, we can encourage people to:

- question conformity wherever they feel it conflicts with their own values; and
- take every opportunity to explore, experiment and practise being as different as they want to be.

In this way it might be possible to achieve a balance between conformity and diversity, a state where we can be as spiky as we want to be and 'fit in' by being different.

CONCLUSION

Although this chapter is entitled 'Working with diversity' it is also about working with conformity. Being highly differentiated when there is a need for conformity is just as inappropriate as burying our differences in a constant need to fit in. It is the dynamic balance which is the key to working with diversity, and it is through seeking this dynamic balance that we find unity.

4 Levels of diversity

INTRODUCTION

Diversity can be seen at many levels, from family to tribe to nation to federations of nations. At every level diversity is embedded as a means of bringing groups together in a harmony that depends on diversity. Just as an orchestra of many diverse instruments and diverse musical talents comes together in a harmony that is beautiful and spiritual in its depth, so people of many differences at many levels can come together. Not to be the same, but to welcome and enjoy each other's differences.

LARGE SYSTEMS (WHERE IS THE INDIVIDUAL?)

In large systems, such as global organizations spanning many countries and cultures and with many thousands of employees, recognition and acceptance of diversity is essential. Such organizations operate in many languages, with many currencies and across many frontiers. Diversity is the essence of their success.

Yet it is possible, even probable, that in some of these organizations the underlying philosophy and culture will be to expect people to conform to organizational values and patterns of behaviour. These are usually espoused by the current top management and may well continue to foster the beliefs of long-dead founders of the business. These values and patterns of behaviour may well have been reasonable in terms of fostering the past growth and development of the business, but can also be socially and ecologically unacceptable at the present time.

Individual values often have to be suppressed in order for people to conform with those espoused by the large system. There is, of course, a measure of choice in the individual's decision to conform, and some people make a conscious choice not to work for organizations whose values they do not and cannot accept. However, many people need to work and are prepared to conform even when their personal values differ from the organization's.

People who work for organizations that manufacture and distribute cigarettes are expected to conform with the dubious values of the organization. Many will be smokers who share the same values, but others will not. This mismatch of values also occurs in oil and timber companies. The sanitized values they display in the West mask the damaging actions of some extraction companies in the developing world. And what of armament manufacturing which creates approximately 400 000 jobs in the UK? No doubt all of these people conform with the values of the organization they work for even if for many of them their own personal values are against war and the arms trade.

Perhaps the power of the pay packet is sufficient to persuade people to conform, when their inner humanity argues against it. Where is the individual's voice in such large systems? Is it drowned out by the sheer weight of conforming numbers so that those who disagree have to do so with their feet and leave to find work elsewhere? The power of large systems is enormous and their demand for conformity is significant.

However, even large systems who are unaware of their dependence on diversity can embrace it and give people more freedom to express themselves and to do things differently. They can achieve this by accepting and understanding that as organizations they exist because of diversity at the small system level. Large systems are always comprised of many smaller systems and it is through these smaller systems that diversity can be fully embraced.

SMALL SYSTEMS (THE INDIVIDUAL EMERGES)

Large organizations consist of smaller companies and/or divisions, which themselves consist of departments and/or teams. It is in these small systems that people function, make relationships and emerge as individuals.

It is in small systems that people have a true sense of belonging. This is the place with which they identify even if they recognize that they are part of something much bigger. The bigger picture is often too remote for most people. Of course people also identify with the image of the bigger entity when they choose to – for example, organizations such as Microsoft and Virgin.

In the small system people are known and their individual differences are experienced by others, and it is here that they strive to fit in. As the notion of teamwork spreads, this identification with the small system will increase and as it does so people face the dilemma of finding the balance between conformity and diversity. All successful teams are able to find this balance and to work with unity.

At the small system level conformity is what bonds the system or team together and diversity is what makes them creative, innovative, exciting and capable of high performance. Too much conformity and the small system becomes a close-knit, cosy, possibly closed group that does not communicate well with other groups and probably performs poorly. Too much diversity and the group loses its shape altogether and the system collapses. What is needed is an appropriate level of diversity that excites and motivates people, and sufficient conformity to provide the cohesiveness essential for the small system to survive.

Appropriate diversity is not a pipedream. It is achievable if people are able to work together because they are different rather than playing down differences.

One powerful exercise for small systems to practise is for each individual in the system to highlight their 'creative difference'. These creative differences, once acknowledged, owned and accepted, can release the small system to really use the potential that exists.

DIVERSITY AND THE INDIVIDUAL

At the individual level diversity takes on another meaning. People tend to reveal only that level of difference that they believe will be tolerated. Tolerance of difference can be very broad or not exist at all. The risk this presents is a constant inner conflict that affects every choice that we make in our lives. Here is an example:

> John is a member of a team of eight people who manage and staff a shoe shop on a busy main street in a large town. John is on duty when a customer returns a pair of shoes which, although sold as a matching pair, are clearly different shades of blue. John is quite clear about replacing the shoes. Unfortunately the shop does not have any more of that size and style and the customer asks for her money back. The company, of which the shop is a branch, have a policy of only replacing goods or issuing credit notes. John decides to give the customer her money back and deal with the consequences later. At a team meeting he reports his action and at first the manager is annoyed and reprimands John, but after some discussion during which the rest of the team support John the manager retracts and the company agree to change the way the branch works in this respect.

In this example John could have conformed with the company policy, but he chose not to and to accept the consequences. In fact his choice to be different influenced the way the group will work in future. Clearly his difference in this situation is something the group can tolerate.

In many organizations the way small systems are allowed to operate is highly constrained by policy, rules and procedures, and individual diversity is frowned on. In such organizations control replaces creativity and such organizations are rarely market leaders or financially successful.

Where small systems/teams are given freedom with responsibility and where

27

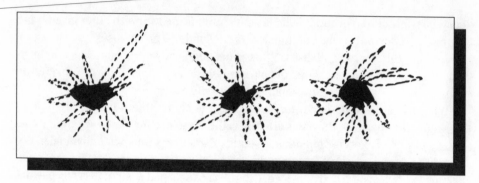

Figure 4.1   Concealing differences

diversity is encouraged the results are amazing. However, individuals will not bring their differences and creativity to the workplace if they feel threatened with being reprimanded or being rejected by colleagues. People tend to play safe when their livelihood is on the line. It takes a brave person to fly in the face of the established procedure. What tends to happen is that we have small systems of people hiding rather than showing their spikes (Figure 4.1).

All this hidden potential unavailable because of the fear created by an organization that does not trust or believe in its people. Sad, but all too true.

APPROPRIATE DIVERSITY

So what is appropriate diversity in the modern organization?

APPROPRIATE DIVERSITY IN LARGE SYSTEMS

Appropriate diversity in large systems means allowing the small systems to operate with freedom and responsibility whilst conforming to the broad vision and values of the large system.

Figure 4.2 represents a simplified view of a large system with three levels of small systems. At each level the small system operates with freedom and responsibility. At the point where the small system connects into the large system there has to be a degree of conformity with the vision and values of the larger system of which it is a part. This larger system can itself operate with freedom and responsibility and in turn needs to conform with the expectations of the even larger system. In this way diversity and conformity can exist side by side in a highly flexible and creative way.

A very large organization with five levels in its structure decided to standardize its management information systems. After a study had been completed the

28

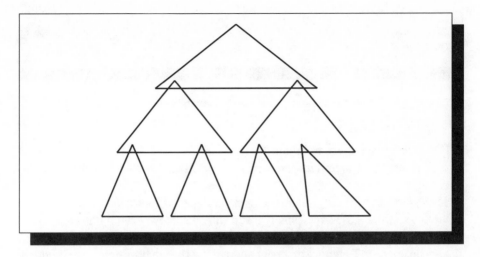

Figure 4.2   Appropriate diversity in large systems

consultants recommended that each small system could operate its own appropriate system to meet its specific needs as long as it transferred essential information upwards in a form that could be easily consolidated. Top management resisted this proposal but agreed to experiment with a pilot in one part of the business. The pilot was so successful that the scheme was quickly extended. Not only were the individual small system needs more appropriately met but the cost of doing so was considerably less than the alternative 'grand strategy'.

APPROPRIATE DIVERSITY IN SMALL SYSTEMS

Appropriate diversity in small systems involves allowing individuals to operate with personal freedom and responsibility whilst conforming to the values and principles that underlie the way the group/team have agreed to operate and at the same time continually questioning them. This permissive attitude also enables new members of a team to establish a place for themselves and their differences in the team.

Small systems change in their personal membership in a more noticeable way than large systems. That is to say that people leaving and joining small systems have a greater impact on the small system than they do on the large system. This in turn can have a different scale of result depending upon to what extent the group can tolerate difference.

If, for example, the small system is a highly conforming group who strongly resist change and defend the *status quo* then newcomers will need to spend time learning how to fit in and probably withdraw their spikes completely – in other words the tolerance for difference is low.

29

Figure 4.3   The 'diversity tolerance' continuum

If the group are more open and welcome difference and explore how differences brought by newcomers can expand the group, then the tolerance for difference is high.

This range of 'diversity tolerance' can be depicted as a continuum with two polarities (Figure 4.3). Every small group will sit somewhere on this continuum, depending on the people who make up the group and the environment in which the group operate. To ignore diversity tolerance at the small system level is both to deny reality and to risk either being rejected or destroying the system. Small systems are notoriously good at avoiding self-destruction.

A medium-sized company that was growing quickly was influenced to a major extent by the current chief executive who was the founder of the business. He decided he needed to hand over responsibility for day-to-day management to a senior manager whom he trusted. She did not operate in the same way as her boss, but she had always conformed with his way of working, never risking to show her differences. In her new position she decided to assert herself and to allow some of her spikes to appear. She did this in quite an aggressive way. Having misjudged the level of 'diversity tolerance' she was strongly resisted by her colleagues and the cohesiveness of the senior management team disintegrated. This resulted in her leaving the company. In subsequent counselling she discovered that it might have been a better course of action to have tested the 'diversity tolerance' with a little more care and to reveal her spikiness with less abandon.

APPROPRIATE DIVERSITY FOR INDIVIDUALS

Appropriate diversity for individuals means behaving in a way which honours individual values and beliefs and constantly questions the values, beliefs and working practices of the small system of which the individual is a part, whilst conforming to a level that does not threaten the individual's sense of belonging to the group.

Finding this balance between conforming and being different is never easy. If you imagine a personal continuum that goes from being highly conforming to being highly differentiated, then you will probably recognize that you have a tendency to act from one main starting point on this continuum (Figure 4.4).

Figure 4.4   Personal conformity–diversity continuum

Finding a balance does not mean sitting in the middle, as many people do, it means moving up and down the continuum as the situation and environment seem to require. This is what is difficult. It is made even more difficult if you do not have any idea of the 'diversity tolerance' of the small system to which you belong.

As most people belong to more than one small system – for example family, work group and soccer team – where the 'diversity tolerances' are different, the constant search for the right place to be on the continuum can become a burden, and it becomes easier to move to the end of the continuum where we feel 'most at home'. We can also operate at either end of the continuum in passive or active ways. For example, you might choose to conform by either 'going along with' or 'demanding conformity from' others. Similarly you could differentiate by 'withdrawing from the group', or alternatively being vocally and/or physically 'very different'.

CONCLUSION

Finding appropriate diversity at an individual level is where people struggle to really 'know themselves'. A strong sense of self-image is important in making the choices necessary to discover 'appropriate diversity' at a personal level. In a society and in organizations which demand conformity it is very hard to establish a strong sense of self simply because to do so we have to be ourselves with all our spikes on display.

5 Intervening in large systems

INTRODUCTION

Most organizations operate as large systems, with a primary aim of staying intact and connected. They do this by establishing structures, methodologies, rules and procedures that seek to ensure:

- continuity of the organization as it is;
- consistency in the way things are done;
- stability in the sense of creating order out of chaos.

All of these are difficult if not impossible to achieve because the world is a constantly changing place where nothing does or can stay the same. So an illusion of sameness is created by establishing patterns of behaviour with which people are encouraged and expected to conform.

'THE WAY WE DO THINGS HERE'

Modern organizations are full of standards, rules, controls and limits, often enshrined in voluminous operating and/or procedure manuals. These documents have grown out of a need to encode the culture that has developed over a long period of time. They are constantly added to and it is rare to find any serious attempts to delete old out-of-date practices.

A large organization in the financial services sector started a project to examine the possibility of putting the seven volumes of operating procedures on-line using CD roms. The consultants involved recommended that this would only serve to maintain the present practices, many of which were obsolete. They suggested that the operating procedures were rewritten in a way that could fully utilize the latest technology and be of current relevance to an organization that was changing rapidly. This was too radical and there are now nine volumes on CD rom.

Very few organizations document their culture as such, yet a culture exists that has a very powerful influence on what people do and the way they do things. Even when top management changes and people come in from the outside the existing culture still plays a significant part in what happens. Organizational culture is very hard to shift no matter how this is attempted.

WHAT IS CULTURE?

Culture can be described as published and espoused beliefs, values and norms driving organizational behaviour, together with unpublished or covert assumptions, values and norms. These two aspects of an organization's culture can sometimes conflict. People say they believe one thing but their behaviour indicates that they believe something else.

The four elements of culture are:

- shared assumptions and beliefs ⎫
- shared values   ⎬   The *thinking* side
- shared norms ⎫
- shared patterns of behaviour ⎬   The *doing* side

ASSUMPTIONS AND BELIEFS

These are the deepest part of an organization's culture. Some of them are stated and some – probably most – are not. People learn them from experience from their peers and from their 'leaders', and in turn become carriers of the culture.

VALUES

These are ideas which the organization values and which are the criteria for making decisions and driving behaviour. Here are two examples:

- The customer is king.
- The bottom line rules round here.

When people share the same personal values and beliefs as those espoused by the organization they will work to reinforce the culture which carries these values. It will seem that they can operate as part of the larger system without feeling that they are in any way denying their own individuality. They are conforming because they agree with the organization's value system. This level of conforming may be conscious or unconscious, but either way people do not have any sense of conflict with the organization's culture.

When people find that their personal values conflict with those of the organization there is discomfort. A dichotomy arises as to whether people conform regardless or question the culture.

In one large organization a management conference to examine cultural problems asked managers to work in four groups:

- *rebels* – what we want to change is ...
- *establishment* – what we want to strengthen is ...
- *status quo* – what we want to keep the same is ...
- *the shadow* – what we know about our culture but never say is ...

What the managers discovered was that there were many aspects of the existing culture that they valued and wanted to keep, and this surprised them. They had all been focusing on what they didn't like and didn't agree with.

What tends to happen is that aspects of the organization's values which conflict with personal values grow until the level of discomfort impinges on individual and organizational performance. At this point nothing the organization espouses seems to satisfy its people. The example of the conference described above shows that there is nearly always a mixture of values and beliefs both acceptable and desirable and unacceptable.

NORMS

The oughts, shoulds, musts, do's, don'ts, standards, policies, rules, procedures, regulations, principles, laws and taboos are all norms that have come to be part of 'the way we do things here'.

A belief generates a value which drives a norm:

- **Belief**   Bosses don't like bad news and punish the bearers.
- **Value**   Personal security.
- **Norm**   If anything goes wrong, look the other way or don't tell anyone.

Some norms are documented, but most are not and are learned through observing peer and leadership behaviour. The initial temptation for new people is to conform with the norms so as to be seen to 'fit in', to belong, to be accepted, regardless of whether people agree with the beliefs and values which the norms imply.

A small company wanted to ensure it was able to keep its 'family values' as it grew. The exercise carried out by consultants showed that everyone was focusing on the 'good' family values and that nobody was paying attention to the shadow side. What emerged was that there were two norms that were interfering with the way the company performed, both seen as 'family values' but not talked about. These were: conflict is not welcome; and don't rock the boat.

PATTERNS OF BEHAVIOUR

Patterns of behaviour are *habitual* ways of carrying out organizational, managerial, supervisory and leadership tasks and activities. Patterns of behaviour that reflect a culture which serves the organization would have these characteristics:

- **Strategy**   Clear-cut focus.
- **Operations**   Effective working procedures and programmes leading to high-quality products and services.
- **Structures**   Optimizing information-sharing, decision-making and workflow.
- **Flexible jobs**   Offering the opportunity and support to add value.
- **Informed teams**   All the information needed to support high performance would be readily available.
- **Performance management**   The right people in the right jobs measured and rewarded accordingly.
- **Management**   Helping people to give their best.
- **Leadership**   Enhancing innovation and change.

A STRONG CULTURE

A strong culture which enables people to make choices about the extent to which they conform and/or ask questions – that is, to discover their level of 'appropriate diversity' – is one that has the following attributes:

- A well-defined set of beliefs, values and norms are firmly in place.
- The beliefs, values and norms are shared by a critical mass of people.
- The shared norms consistently drive behaviour.
- The resulting patterns of behaviour resist forces of change over time.

Some people find that organizations which have a strong culture demand conformity, but often organizations with a strong culture are more able to embrace diversity because they are not threatened by it.

THE SHADOW SIDE OF CULTURE

The shadow side of the espoused culture lies in an organization's failure to get its publicly endorsed beliefs, values and norms to drive behaviour. Fanciful espoused values give way, in practice, to the real values, the ones the organization uses.

Actual patterns of behaviour tell us what the organization really believes, prizes, encourages and sanctions.

ADAPTIVE CULTURES

Culture should be strong and flexible. This requires everyone in the organization to pay attention to 'what is going on' and to adapt their beliefs, values, norms and behaviour accordingly. Adaptive cultures are:

- **vigilant** – scanning the horizon for opportunities and threats;
- **proactive** – in moving towards their vision rather than reactive to events;
- able to **let go** – particularly of the past, and know what to keep;
- **modern** – but not falling victim to fads. They continually reassess.

Adaptive cultures are constantly aware of how the culture is serving the organization and ready and willing to change to align the culture with the needs of the organization.

STEPPING OUT OF LINE

The expression 'stepping out of line' seems to echo the desirability of people staying in line and not being 'out of step' with everyone else. Our language is littered with such expressions. In large systems, when people are dissatisfied with how things are, they can choose to 'step out of line' and to say what they think. This is a courageous choice for most people and means taking a big risk.

SO WHY TAKE THE RISK?

Stepping out of line is not necessarily a good large-system intervention. The impact can be minimal for the extent of the personal effort and the effort can have consequences for the individual out of all proportion to the value generated. It is not a surprise, therefore, that few people take this option. 'What's the point? Nobody listens and I am just one voice.'

THE DISAPPEARING INDIVIDUAL

If nobody listens when people step out of line then it is as if they do not exist. Individuals disappear all the time in large organizations. Some disappear by leaving and some disappear by staying. From being a spiky individual the disappearing individual becomes an amorphous blob, a part of 'the employees' or 'the workforce' or of the organization's 'human resources'.

There are millions and millions of people who leave their homes as highly visible fathers, mothers, wives, husbands, partners, sons or daughters, only to enter the organization and to disappear as individuals. In these organizations employee numbers are more important than names; titles are used to define roles rather than names that say 'here we are'.

HELL

Serried ranks of sombre men
on the early morning train awake.
Tired and lonely they sit and muse,
reading pages of dismal news.
The mood's depressing.
Not a smile in sight.
They follow a pattern, long been set,
working hard until they get
the rewards they've long toiled for.
Time is precious. They fill it well.
Making each day a living hell.
I find it sad. I know for me
that this is not the way to be.
So while I'm with them once again,
I have the time to sit and think
and recognize the pain.
My life is now too full of joy,
to return to the daily toil.
I'll not miss the ranks of sombre men,
for now I'm happy all the time,
instead of just now and then.

By Trevor Bentley

CELEBRATING AND VALUING INDIVIDUALITY

A large organization had performed poorly in terms of profit, and needed to boost profits. The top management team nominated four of its members to study the problem and come up with a solution. The organization employed 11 000 people. The solution they came up with was to reduce the workforce by 10 per cent, which would produce the required boost to profits.

The result was indeed a short-term boost to profits, followed by a subsequent decline as service and quality fell off. A new chief executive was appointed. This time instead of nominating a small management team to look at the problem he asked all the people working for the organization, now 10 000, to think about and discuss with each other how the business could be more successful. His strategy paid off handsomely and the organization prospered. When asked about his strategy the chief executive said, 'Why rely on four people to find a solution when I can call on the creativity of 10 000?'

When people are allowed to disappear in large systems they take with them all their creativity and potential. Only by seeing people as individuals and recognizing that they have a view of what is happening, and probably know better than anyone at the top what is going on, can organizations prosper. So one of the primary large-system interventions is to stop people from disappearing.

Asian Business magazine reported the story of Eric Chia, the Chinese businessman who was brought in to rescue the Malaysian state-owned Perwaja Steel which was in a very poor condition. Talking about how he did this he said:

> 'So the first thing I did at Perwaja was to find out if the problems were technical, human, managerial or financial. I would sit down low at the back of the guardhouse near the entrance gate. I wanted to see how the people behaved. I found that in the morning the gate was too big and in the evening it was too small. So I said to myself, people don't like to work here. They come to work with their body but they keep their soul at home. Therefore it was a people problem.'

He then set about talking to everyone in groups, departments and sections. His aim was, in his own words:

> 'I wanted to find out what I could do for them, not what they must do for me.'

He talked to every individual, asking them: How did you come to Perwaja? What were you before? Where is your rainbow? He told them about his own background, since he wanted them to feel that he was one of them. His approach had remarkable results. (Bedi 1995, pp. 42–4)

CREATIVITY AND THE EXCITEMENT OF QUESTIONING EVERYTHING

Creativity flows from diversity. People are most creative at the limits of their spikiness. Here at the boundaries where people push against their world is a place of adventure and excitement. Anything is possible. In cultures of conformity, on the other hand, creativity is stifled. We cannot be creative when we have to follow values we do not believe in and 'fit in'. Creativity comes from being different.

Management who seek conformity from their staff can be extremely challenged and frustrated when people constantly question 'Why do we do things like that here?' The answers that are forthcoming can include rational and justifiable reasons and the questioners are satisfied, but all too often the answers are more in line with 'Because that's how we do things here', as if this is sufficient reason, and the message about not questioning is clear. If people continue to question they can be branded as 'troublemakers' and become isolated and belittled. It takes courage to continue to ask questions, and creativity is all about asking questions.

When organizations encourage and foster the exciting prospect of 'questioning everything' they release the floodgates of creativity and never look back. Productivity and efficiency both increase and people find work more exciting and fun and they no longer disappear.

IS CULTURE CHANGE POSSIBLE?

Why do cultures need to change? Because they no longer serve the organization. How do we know? Because there are many difficulties and intractable problems and a high degree of disharmony with a fall-off in the quality of performance. Can cultures be changed? Yes, they can – British Airways changed a culture of indifference and arrogance to one of service.

How far and deep do such changes need to go? They can transform the organization's personality, a process which is a long-term and painful road to travel. Or they can change patterns of behaviour, a less painful and short-term route.

A THREE-STAGE APPROACH TO CULTURE CHANGE

The following suggestion for a three-stage approach may seem, at first sight, quite straightforward. However, it will call for a considerable commitment over a long period to achieve any really worthwhile change. The three stages are:

● auditing the culture to decide what to change;
● developing the beliefs, values and norms of the preferred culture;
● determining culture change strategies that fit the organization.

AUDITING THE CULTURE

The culture audit involves meeting with people to discover the following:

● Identify key shared assumptions, beliefs, values and norms, especially covert ones.
● Identify organization-limiting patterns of behaviour that these generate.
● Determine what keeps these patterns of behaviour in place.

Some of the questions that need to be asked are: What norms interfere with performance? How does the organization keep dysfunctional elements in place? What recurring and/or intractable problems exist? Answers to these questions are windows into the culture of the organization.

People are the carriers of culture

Because much of the culture is unwritten it has to be carried by the people. Just as in years gone by people learned about their heritage from the stories and ballads of their time, so today culture is part and parcel of the human fabric of the organization. Some ways in which this happens are:

- punishing unwanted behaviours (behaviours that are punished are deemed undesirable);
- rewarding desirable behaviours (behaviours that are rewarded are deemed to be desirable);
- staff locked into habit and inertia;
- cloning, by hiring people who fit, and people modelling themselves on their leaders;
- the politics of self-interest.

ESTABLISHING THE PREFERRED CULTURE

The exact way that any organization will set about establishing its preferred culture will depend on the organization and its current culture. Here are some of the steps that can be followed:

- Envisioning where we are going, our aspirations and desires.
- What are our current needs?
- What patterns of behaviour should be in place to meet these needs?
- What beliefs, values and norms are needed to drive these patterns of behaviour?
- Challenge 'the way we do things here'.
- Change to adapting and doing things differently all the time.
- Promote managers because they are good managers, not because they are good at their existing job.

DEVELOPING CULTURE CHANGE STRATEGIES

Successful culture change calls for leadership and commitment from senior managers, more because the latter are seen as models than because they tell people what to do. Modelling culture change involves managers taking every opportunity to stress the new behaviours by:

- using new beginnings;
- using crises;
- mandating the preferred culture;

- asking in what way does the preferred culture
  - expand people?
  - limit people?

The beliefs, values and norms that drive how people relate to each other are crucial. So it is necessary to look at forms of relationships that serve the organization, and those that do not.

SIX WAYS TO INTERVENE IN LARGE SYSTEMS

These are not the only ways in which you can intervene in large systems, but they are ways that can prove particularly successful in helping organizations change cultures of conformity into cultures of diversity:

- Changing places.
- Listen to the people you don't normally listen to.
- Focus on relationships.
- Examine contact boundaries.
- Experiment.
- Send out 'invitations to the ball'.

CHANGING PLACES

Top management can spend some time actually changing places with staff for a day. Experience what they experience every day and let them experience what you experience, then compare notes and change what can be changed for the better. Ask your CEO to change places with you for the day. Take the risk of asking and take the risk of actually doing it. The results from changing places when it is a regular and widespread part of the culture are extraordinary.

LISTEN TO THE PEOPLE YOU DON'T NORMALLY LISTEN TO

People working in large systems usually have a surprisingly narrow group of people they normally listen to. This is particularly true of top management. The first step is to list the people to whom you do normally listen and see just how limited your range of hearing is. Then list the people you never hear and set about making sure you create the opportunity to listen to them. As with changing places this intervention can be amazing in the extent and scope of what comes from 'extended listening'.

FOCUS ON RELATIONSHIPS

When people meet in large systems they rarely meet as 'you and me'. What usually happens is that they meet as roles, for example Head of Research or Chief Accountant. Like two actors on the stage they play their part and follow their lines and never meet as real people, but as roles, often in full costume.

When people meet at the 'you and me' level they are themselves. They are interested in each other as people not as titles. The focus becomes a 'real' relationship. Issues such as why they like or dislike each other, or why they compete rather than cooperate, how many kids they have, and so on, become more important than the occupational reason for them to meet.

For this to happen everyone has to bring a loving TOUCH to their work, where TOUCH stands for Trust, Openness, Understanding, Consideration and Honesty. In many organizations this is to fly in the face of the current culture where personal issues and emotions are parked at the front door when people enter. And even in organizations that encourage real relationships there will be people who prefer to keep their personal lives to themselves and who choose to meet at the role level. In such cases their personal choice should be respected rather than demand they conform to a level of contact they do not want.

EXAMINE CONTACT BOUNDARIES

If an organization encourages its people to be individual and spiky then contact boundaries become where their spikes touch, or at their growing edges. This is not always a safe place for people to make contact with others. Two people exploring their limits will be vulnerable and at risk. It is important then that people can establish and communicate clear contact boundaries.

Sexual harassment is one area where clear contact boundaries have not been established. Setting clear contact boundaries means three things. First, being aware of what is a 'comfortable' boundary with others, and of course this can change from person to person. However, if people are not clear themselves about their own contact boundaries there is a distinct risk of them unconsciously giving out 'inappropriate' signals.

Secondly, people need to be able to state what is and what is not comfortable for them in direct, precise language. 'I do not want you to touch me' and 'I do not want you to call me "love"' are two examples. Thirdly, it is important that people always state when their boundaries have been invaded even if this causes them only the slightest discomfort.

By paying attention to contact boundaries in this way everyone is able to operate within their own comfort zone and make contact only at the contact zone of others.

EXPERIMENT

Trying things out is experimenting. Seeing what happens is one of the best ways to discover what is possible. It is risky and exciting. When people are encouraged to experiment it means they can explore the outer reaches of their spikiness and by so doing become highly creative.

Experimenting means that people cannot get it wrong. When the outcome of an experiment is not what we expect it might be, it is not a mistake but an interesting outcome from which we can learn. Another way of saying this is that mistakes are a basis for learning and not a reason for punishment.

SEND OUT 'INVITATIONS TO THE BALL'

When Cinderella did not receive an invitation to the ball she needed a fairy godmother to get her in. It is possible to make sure that everyone gets an invitation to the ball. In other words every organization needs its own fairy godmother.

This large-system intervention is often known as participation and/or involvement, but is more often than not a process of 'paying lip service' to the notion of involvement, and only the Ugly Sisters get invited. Inviting everyone to the ball means just that. There are no Cinderellas: everyone has the opportunity to 'be there', to say what they think and to play as much a part in events as everyone else.

The ball could be a large gathering of all staff, or smaller gatherings on a local basis, or a less personal gathering of ideas through a staff survey, or permanent continuing opportunities to contribute to the organization's thinking through learning/discovery groups.

All of these invitations are intended to adjust the culture to one that is more attentive to individuals and their ideas. By doing this the culture can take on the values of all staff rather than just those emanating from the top.

CONCLUSION

All large-system interventions require individual action and attention to 'making things happen'. Any large-system intervention which does not have this individual flavour will damage rather then benefit the organization.

REFERENCE

Bedi, Hari (1995), 'There can be only one tiger', *Asian Business*, Vol. 31, No. 3.

6   Intervening in small systems

INTRODUCTION

We are born into a world of small systems. The life that we know best is a life of interacting small systems: families, schools, clubs, at work, even 'the local' can provide important social systems in a community. In the workplace you might be in a department, work in a team or project group, be involved in specialist function groups, or belong to specific work groups like quality circles. Not only are these small systems defined by their particular functions, they are also affected and bounded by time; for example, family groups are defined by their members' life span, small groups in organizations exist for a limited time only.

All of these systems are places in which we learn and make meaning of our lives. A key function of small systems is that they provide a place where people can find a sense of belonging. In organizations another function of small systems is to draw on the collective potential of the employees – although it has never been expressed in this way. Like fish, who are oblivious to the water in which they swim, we are so often oblivious to the existence of this life-sustaining aspect of the environment on which we depend. Small systems form the infrastructure of human life. We co-create systems – we *are* small systems.

DIVERSITY AND SMALL SYSTEMS IN ORGANIZATIONS

The 'appropriate diversity' of small systems is as important in organizations as the 'appropriate diversity' of large systems and of individuals, both of which have already been explained in Chapter 4. Here we explore how to engage with the diversity of small systems and make interventions that will support this process; how to build healthy connections between these small systems in the light of their difference, and how to maintain an appropriate diversity within the context of the business.

SMALL SYSTEMS IN ORGANIZATIONS

The small systems and subsystems of an organization can range from a small group of two or three people, to operational teams, project groups, sales teams, management teams, a whole division, and so on. These small systems do not operate in isolation but are influenced by the culture of the organization, and through their interactions with each other will in turn impact on the culture of the organization. Groups and teams are crucial to the way we operate in organizations; they help us think in terms of the whole organization and they create the infrastructures for running a business. Thinking in terms of small systems enables leaders to make sense of the contribution that 500, 1000 or even 12 000 employees give to a business. Organizational structures *are* small systems.

THE PROFILE OF A SMALL SYSTEM

The *identity* of a small system is gained first through its title and purpose, and secondly through the collective personalities, group dynamics and underlying motivations of its members. The title should capture the business purpose of the group or team – what they are here to do. In many groups the members will find common ground through a collective purpose that supports and sometimes goes beyond the business need. In addition, like people, groups find their identity through their interactions with the wider system. So the diversity of a small system is established in many ways:

- through its business purpose;
- through the interactions between its members;
- through a collective purpose;
- through its connection with the wider system/s in which it exists;
- through its relationship with other small systems.

Through its identity a small system will also establish its boundary, the critical quality necessary for inter-group diversity.

COLLECTIVE PURPOSE

Collective purpose is, if you like, people connecting through discovering similarities in one of their spikes – not all. This is unity through connecting a common link in one spike and retaining uniqueness in the rest of the spikes (Figure 6.1).

Common purpose acts as a control mechanism – it prevents anarchy and sets up a healthy, productive tension between diversity and unity. The purpose must be defined by the group, it is the roots of belonging. When these roots are strong and visible to the world people join because they identify with these roots – for instance

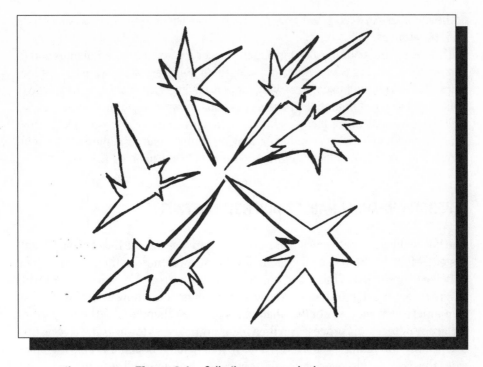

Figure 6.1   Collective purpose and uniqueness

environmental groups, quality groups. When purpose is established the freedom for individuals to do things differently and to be different can occur. Co-creation of the group takes place. Members of the group can allow their self-identity to emerge, and in so doing relationships within the group develop. Self-identity (discussed in more depth in Chapter 7) is a process of creating self-boundaries and self-definition.

BOUNDARIES

> The exasperating fact which Adam learned was that every boundary line is also a potential battle line, so that just to draw a boundary is to prepare one's self for conflict. (Wilber 1979, p. 19)

A boundary provides the definition for a group to have a sense of itself as an entity capable of acting as a whole. Only then is it able to differentiate itself from other groups. In order to have a sense of itself a group must be able to see multiple possibilities within itself. Group members therefore must practise diversity in the way they relate to each other, in order to know the full range of possibilities available. Diversity between small systems is therefore dependent on the self-identity of the members in each small system, and the capacity of members to appreciate their differences.

The clearer the boundary of a group the easier it is to build relationships and to appreciate the diversity of other groups. Without boundaries there are no relationships, there is nothing to connect with, there is no diversity to practise and there is limited releasing of potential. However, as soon as we determine boundaries we face the possibility of conflict – and that poses a problem for many people. People tend to be better skilled at avoiding or denying conflict than managing it in a useful and productive way. Conflict is addressed more fully in Chapter 14.

DIVERSITY WITHIN ENABLES DIVERSITY BETWEEN

The key to diversity between small systems has to begin at the heart of each small system. Members of the small system develop an awareness of their own patterns of behaviour and learn the art of building relationships and how to connect with others through being different. Above all they must learn how to deal with their own differences and the conflict that exists between them. Given the purpose of the group or team this process can then naturally progress towards the co-creation of a healthy, integrated system with a fairly well-defined boundary. This then provides the basis for discovering the differences with other small systems.

HEALTHY FUNCTIONING OF A SMALL SYSTEM

What do we mean by the healthy functioning of a small system and what is the relevance of this to diversity?

Theories of good functioning are just theories; the qualities of a healthy group or team – for example challenging, rich awareness, valuing difference, managing conflict, and so on – are not always present. Accepting that chaos is at times inevitable, that skills and abilities for healthy group functioning are not fully developed, and believing that the team are capable of working through chaos can be more important than chasing the ideal. However, we can make some assumptions about small systems and how we can intervene in a way that improves the health of the system to support diversity. Figure 6.2 illustrates this point and is developed from the works of Edwin C. Nevis. The freedom to do things differently and to be different are at the core of a healthy system.

POSITIVE ENERGY IN SMALL SYSTEMS

Paying attention to energy changes and interpretations of energies is a useful skill in promoting diversity in small systems.

Assumptions	Observations
1 A healthy system supports itself by knowing what it does well.	Groups and teams are often unaware of what they do well. Helping a team to see what it is that they do well leads to a clear identity of themselves and more defined boundaries. This process will also begin to tap into the collective potential of the group.
2 Healthy systems exist in a state of flux.	Groups and teams are not fixed entities, they fluctuate with the tide of change within the larger system. That means that the diversity within the system, the diversity of the system, and the potential floating around the system also fluctuate. This can provide positive and exciting energy for a team and prevent it becoming bogged down with fixed patterns of behaviour.
3 Each system is as unique as each individual member.	An awareness of the group's dynamics can be a stimulus for challenging behaviours that undermine diversity, such as prejudices or pulling the group towards conformity. For example, you might notice someone reacting too quickly to a comment or opinion, or realize that you personally are convinced that you know what is good for the group without taking time to observe or ask questions.
4 The well-being of subsystems is important to the well-being of the whole system.	Subsystems aid the functioning of the whole system, a bit like the organs of the body. Subsystems are not in themselves a whole organism but are important to the functioning of the whole organism, as kidneys or the liver are to the human organism. These subsystems will, through the very nature of their functioning, be diverse albeit that they retain at their core the purpose of the whole system. Amplifying the diversity of subsystems will contribute to the healthy diversity of the whole system.
5 Some subsystems create a lot of energy and other subsystems have little energy.	It is tempting to direct attention to the subsystem creating the most energy. Do not be seduced away from subsystems that show little energy. A system diminishes its collective potential if it puts a value judgement on energy levels, for two reasons: ● The essence of diversity is in recognizing what is, rather than rejecting what is not. ● When little energy flows it might be that potential has become stuck, so extra attention, as opposed to reduced attention, is needed.

Figure 6.2 Observations on the five basic assumptions of the healthy functioning of small systems

In physics energy has positive and negative qualities in it. An example of this to which we can all relate is that of a simple torch battery, which has positive and negative poles. When these poles connect through the environment, the battery releases its energy. A battery alone does nothing: it is only when it is put into a torch (interacting with the environment) that it can create light. People are just the same, and in behavioural terms these two poles are sometimes referred to as the light and the shadow. Light is often taken to represent positive behaviours, for instance unconditional love, caring, respect, forgiveness, compassion; shadow often to represent the dark side of human nature, the negative and sometimes destructive side of our existence, for example hate, anger, fear and vengeance. Energy is released when these poles interact with the environment.

In a battery, if there is a bad contact at either the positive or negative pole, there is no outcome, no consequence, no effect. This is also true of people – we need another person with whom to connect. How we connect with the other person influences our energy and our response, for positive or negative. If there is no contact there is no response.

Where is all this leading to? Well, when we address diversity we touch the very edge of our shadow. We begin to experience the polarities in society, in our systems, most of all in the small systems that are so important to us. Like the battery it is only when these opposites, both positive and negative, interact with the environment (the observer or the recipient) that they have an effect.

We live in a world of opposites. These opposites co-exist. You cannot have one without the other, for the one helps to define the other. Some examples of common opposites follow:

love	hate
happy	sad
life	death
intelligent	stupid
beautiful	ugly
good	evil
pleasure	pain
freedom	bondage
success	failure
strong	weak

Historically we have found the comfort of light in conformity, which is a way of denying that the shadow exists. Diversity and unity construct a different paradigm, one in which we begin to learn of the polarities that exist in human nature. Our task is to learn how to shine the light; that is, how to engage with the interaction between opposites, usefully. When love and hate are in the arena, how can we build on love and not deny the hate? When success and failure are present together, how can we push towards success and accept possible failure? When intelligence and stupidity stand in front of us, how can we recognize our own intelligence and face our own stupidity?

What gives power its charge, positive or negative, is the quality of relationships. (Wheatley 1992, p. 39)

When pushing the boundaries of diversity, how can we turn discrimination into differentiation, oppression into release, conformity into diversity? This is the challenge we all face. There are two dimensions here, the exhibited behaviour and the recipient's interpretation of that behaviour. The dynamic is more complex than it seems. We see the world through our own individuality, through our own diversity; the question then is who is shining the light on whom?

Recognizing negative energies

Notice when you:

1 React quickly to a comment or opinion.
2 Have strong feelings about a group member.
3 Are convinced as to what is 'good' for a given group member without taking time to observe them, ask them questions and find out about their competence, shortcomings and history.
4 Take a rigid stance with other group members without considering other people's point of view.
5 Are over-tolerant of abusive or aggressive behaviour.

Supporting others in your team

1 Shadow and light energies carry emotions; the task is to access or shift these emotions when they are inappropriate. Awareness-raising observations are very powerful in promoting emotional shifts: 'I notice that you all seem to get on very well, but what seems to be missing is disagreement or challenge between you.'
2 Where there is denial of the shadow raise it as a possibility: 'You all seem convinced that you will succeed; what would it mean to fail?'
3 Where there is blame, for example towards senior management, get the team to see how they have contributed to the issue, or ask them to be specific and to seek constructive solutions. 'Who in particular do you believe has stopped you from moving forward? What do you need to do in order to re-establish your position?'
4 Where there is prejudice, raise their awareness of the assumptions they are making and how they would feel if they discovered that their assumptions were not true. In extreme cases gentle nudging rather than full-blown challenges are more likely to be effective.

DIVERSITY BETWEEN SMALL SYSTEMS

Diversity between groups, teams, divisions, and so on in an organization occurs mainly through individuals. Rarely do groups and teams meet face to face. Occasionally project teams might come together through the interface of their projects to build on the work that they are doing. Sometimes purchaser–provider teams will meet to establish productive ways of working together – to find win–win outcomes. These meetings tend to be infrequent.

In theory the diversity between small systems grows with increasing awareness of the identity of each small system. Diversity and identity are integrated parts of the same process. That process is interactive both within and between small systems. But what happens in practice?

Diversity between small systems mainly occurs through the individual members of the group who carry the group diversity within them throughout the workplace. There are specific points of contact that vary according to the structure of the organization. These points of contact can be both formal and informal. The team or group identity must be clear to its members for individuals to interact effectively at these points of contact. Without this clarity the rest of the organization could receive mixed or confused messages, resulting in a weak identity for that group and limited opportunity for the potential of the group to be released. With a weak identity it then becomes difficult for other small groups to connect and to build on their potential – so the group becomes even weaker.

Where there is clear identity carried by individual members then it is through their interaction with individuals of other groups that they spark off innovation, creativity and new ideas, and build on the potential of the organization for the business. This is somewhat like bees collecting pollen: by interacting with each other through a ritual dance, they let other groups of bees know where the abundant pollen is and thus work together for the benefit of the hive and their survival, drawing on each other's potential.

MAINTAINING APPROPRIATE DIVERSITY IN THE WIDER SYSTEM

There are two issues here that a small system must take into consideration:

- the diversity tolerance of their own system;
- the diversity tolerance of the wider system in which they operate.

Both of these are like pendulums, constantly moving, continuously changing.

What is important here is that to some extent people are able to predict other people's responses. This means being able to experiment, test, stretch boundaries and if necessary 'pull back' if diversity tolerance is low. Perhaps the term to use is 'acting with intelligence'. That is, using *all* your senses – including common sense – to assess the situation and respond in a way that both supports yourself and others, as well as stretching the boundaries that need pushing out: your boundaries *in* the group, and the boundaries *of* the group.

CONCLUSION

This chapter has been about intervening in small systems to bring diversity to the surface, and about drawing on the potential of people collectively. We, the authors, have often engaged with managers on a one-to-one basis and been drawn by the potential that they bring to the business, only to see this potential diminish in the company of other managers or their teams. This has happened so often that it has become predictable. An advantage of groups and teams in organizations is that they can release collective potential to achieve more than individuals are able to achieve on their own. And yet individual potential is often hidden in the team, as people withdraw their spikes, possibly fearing that to show too much diversity would lead to their expulsion. Where diversity tolerance is low so is the opportunity for groups to explore their potential; where diversity tolerance is high potential explodes into creativity and innovation.

REFERENCES

Wheatley, Margaret J. (1992), *Leadership and the New Science*, San Francisco: Berrett-Koehler.
Wilber, K. (1979), *No Boundary*, Los Angeles: Center Press.

7 Intervening at the individual level

INTRODUCTION

'Isn't it amazing that of the millions of people living in the world, individually we are so different. Not one of us the same as another. Even identical twins have their differences,' said my mother, as we lazed in the shade watching people stroll by.

We were at a summer arts festival which emphasized cultural difference. There were many different exhibitions, traditional arts from countries around the world. People were different, they looked different. You could see their differences by the clothes they were wearing and the different ways they were responding to the arts, crafts, sunshine and music. I loved the novelty; that is what made the festival so exciting for me.

I reflected on her words. She was talking about the miracle of our uniqueness. My curiosity increased. 'So why is it that people seek to belong by "fitting in", allowing themselves to be moulded into shape, to appear the same as each other, when this vibrancy and colour in difference is so exciting, so alive?'

MULTIPLE REALITIES

Something that we as individuals need to recognize if diversity is to be truly valued is that with any one truth there are a multitude of realities. There will be the objective characteristics of the data, and then there will be your subjective viewpoints, which if examined more closely will offer a number of different perspectives, different realities. Then there will be the viewpoints of all the other people involved and their realities. Our experience of reality is coloured by our mood, past experiences, needs, personal preferences, expectations, attitudes, and so on. There is no one objective truth – only a multitude of subjective perceptions.

This mix is a little like fingerprints: there are no two people the same. Where there is no appreciation of multiple realities – that is, where there is only single-mindedness – the effects can be socially devastating. For example, when people carry prejudices they see the world in a way that confirms their prejudices, like looking through tinted glasses that colour everything you see. When people recognize their prejudices they do not get rid of their beliefs but they become open to the possibilities of seeing the world in a different light. Without this awareness there is little hope.

The fact that multiple realities exist around us all the time does not necessarily help our quest for diversity. We already spend a lot of time making sense of the world in order to follow our own truths. Trying to make sense of other people's truths would appear to complicate this process a thousandfold in a single day. The problem seems too complex to engage in such truth-finding continuously. But maybe this is not our task. Perhaps all we need to know is that multiple realities exist. Without this awareness the trap is that we assume that there is only one single truth, our own, and that everyone else sees the situation in exactly the same way as we do, or should do. What happens then is that we behave in the way that supports our belief, as though it is the only single truth. The outcome can be confusing.

VALUING YOUR OWN DIVERSITY

You discover how you are different from other people through your interactions. The closer and more engaging the interaction, the greater the opportunity for identifying difference at deeper personal levels. What this means is that what you see and hear is not all that there is in difference. In fact, if you assume difference just through what you observe, then your view of others is likely to be narrow and probably contaminated by misassumptions and speculative judgements.

LAYERS OF DIFFERENCE

Imagine you are comparing yourself to another person, looking for differences and similarities – someone that you have recently met. Make a list of all the characteristics that appear similar and all the characteristics that appear different between you.

Now compare yourself with someone that you know intimately. Make a similar list.

You will probably find that the nature of your lists are very different. In the first list your comparisons would have been mainly superficial: type of dress, nationality, age, accent, mannerisms, hair colour. In the second list your comparisons are likely to have reached a deeper level such as emotional characteristics, preferences, discrete behaviours, vulnerability, eccentricities, attitudes, passions, and so on. Being able to differentiate at this deeper level can be complex and stretching, and only happens when relationships are allowed to develop.

GETTING TO KNOW YOU

When people do not know you well they have to speculate in order to know how to relate to you. These speculations are built on the other person's way of working, and their past experiences. Speculations begin a process of differentiation, or, for people who tend to conform, a seeking out of similarities. Rarely are people's speculations correct: we are all so different, so how could they be right? If you act on speculation alone and fail to own the assumptions you make, then developing a relationship can be difficult. It is easy to see how prejudice develops.

The way to correct speculation and assumption is to notice your own assumptions, to become aware of how you stereotype people and to know the prejudices that you carry. Discovering real difference, hearing each other's truth, being open about how you see your differences and similarities and sharing your assumptions about each other allows for misassumptions to be corrected between you, leading to meaningful contact. When you understand other people and they understand you, you can discover how to work together and interact in a way that is useful. Even if you realize through this process that you will never be the best of friends, that is better than being enemies through ignorance.

WORKING WITH BOUNDARIES

Just as the difference between small systems depends on the boundaries they set, so for people difference is about setting clear boundaries between themselves and others. As you create a boundary for yourself so you create the possibility for others to exist around you in their difference, their individuality. Where boundaries meet differences are discovered and unity becomes possible.

The minute a baby is born it begins to draw a boundary of self through the boundary between itself and its mother. The baby cannot exist in isolation. Expression of difference comes from a clear sense of self-identity, and self-identity manifests itself through establishing a sense of separateness between self and other, through good clear boundaries. But there is another ingredient that helps this process. The baby is able to differentiate from itself and its mother when it feels loved, valued and respected as an individual in its own right.

If the mother values herself she will be able to value the baby fully for its self. Mother and baby feel a sense of belonging together, as well as their difference. They create a connectedness, a relationship which is new, a bonding that allows them to discover this sense of belonging over and over again and to appreciate their difference. This is appropriate diversity at work.

These boundaries are not so much about separation. Boundaries allow us to make distinctions from which our identity can emerge and take form. Strong conforming cultures eat away at people's boundaries due to over-identification with another or with the system. Self-identity is diminished and so potential is diminished. Through self-identity we can discover diversity and the joy of co-creation and co-evolving. Diversity holds the potential for organizations to exist and evolve. But can it also support an environment that will fulfil the need for belonging?

The predicament

There is a predicament that we all face in creating and maintaining boundaries. In the last chapter we highlighted the point that a boundary line is also a potential battle line, for the boundary line marks difference, often opposites. If difference appears foreign, alien, strange or unpredictable, it can pose a threat to your life and well-being. The challenge is how can you be sufficiently open to allow difference to unfold and still be self-protecting from a potentially dangerous environment both at the same time?

The critical component here is self-support. The following seven steps will help in managing your own self-support:

1 Make sure that you are breathing deeply and regularly. People often stop breathing when they feel uncomfortable or threatened – there is nothing more life-supporting than simply breathing.
2 Check that you are physically supported – that is, with two feet firmly on the ground, your body held in balance or supported well in your seat.
3 Check out your assumptions about other people and make sure that you correct other people's misassumptions about you.
4 State the obvious: 'You and I are clearly different in our views'.
5 Know that your starting point is one of difference, and trust that along the way you can find connections.
6 Notice how you respond to difficult situations, and reflect on the aptness of your responses. You will in some way contribute to the difficult situations you find yourself in, so changing the way you interact can influence a change in the way that others respond to you.
7 Begin a process of appropriate self-disclosure (described later in this chapter).

THE POWER OF EMOTIONS

Human behaviour is driven by emotions. Few people realize the full impact of this statement. The implications begin to surface when we start to realize that expressing emotions is in many organizations not acceptable. When emotions are denied

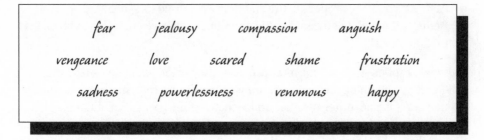

Figure 7.1   Emotions

we exclude crucial information that feeds the very system on which we depend for our survival – and success. Emotions are the bedrock of diversity (Figure 7.1).

A dilemma that we face is how to nourish both *diversity* and *belonging*, both of which carry different sets of emotions, in our search for self-identity. In the Western world, and maybe for the whole world, these two functions of human existence have become polarized and almost incompatible. The pull for many people has been towards belonging, in fear of rejection and the threat of isolation. Here emotions are powerful and compelling. Real isolation means loneliness and loss of self, for we can only gain a sense of self when we are living in relationship with others. Yet paradoxically, conformity (what some people believe to be the act of living in relationship with others) is also a loss of self, because identities merge and boundaries become confused.

For some, survival is about expressing difference, carrying a strong sense of self-identity – the push and pull of emotions here are around fear of loss of independence – or loss of self.

The fear of being alone, rejected, ridiculed and shamed, and the desire to be accepted, valued, recognized and loved, have led many to believe that conformity rather than diversity will fulfil their survival needs. The fear of a loss of boundaries, of being smothered, of loss of difference has led others to believe that eccentricity rather than diversity is how they survive. Yet our fears are often irrational and misperceived, our desires unfulfilled because we fail to make contact with others from a rational place.

MANAGING EMOTIONS

With emotions it can at times be difficult to tell the difference between the rational and the irrational, the real and the imagined. Wherever they come from, emotions are a real experience. What matters is how a person acts and behaves in response to their emotions and this is where the system can fail us:

- Acting through awareness of the emotions that drive us is healthy.
- Acting out of habit and denying the emotions that drive our behaviour can lead to difficulties.

Habitual responses occur out of awareness: they are usually self-sustaining and self-fulfilling, meaning that you see only those things that support your beliefs about yourself and others, rather than challenging them. For example, when people fear rejection it means that they may avoid putting themselves in situations that might lead to them being rejected, like presenting their views on a controversial issue, publicly. The emotions that underlie their fear are very powerful, yet their views are part of their self-identity and help define their personal boundaries.

Building diversity means making sense of your emotions and understanding the deeper meaning behind your feelings and your behaviour, especially when there is no apparent rationale behind what you feel. This can lead to the feeling of rejection being disproportionate to the situation.

It is only by understanding these disproportionate responses that we can begin to truly understand ourselves and discover the boundaries through which our differences can safely emerge.

EMOTIONS IN TEAMS

Helping teams to understand the emotions that create the ebb and flow of their work together can be a very effective way of enabling people to understand themselves in relation to others. A simple exercise that Susan Clayton used with a team recently proved to be an excellent tool for achieving both:

1   She invited the team to name as many specific qualities and attributes that they could think of, or imagine, that create a caring and supportive team.

They came up with examples such as: conflict is dealt with openly; in times of difficulty someone always offers support; people are encouraged to face their challenges; openness (people are open about those things that they fear in themselves); supportive challenge; it's okay to get it wrong; healthy competition; mutual respect; regular contact between team members (not just about business); people simply show they care without having to be prompted.

2   Sue then asked them to come up with behaviours that they know of, or imagine would exist, in a team that is uncaring and unsupportive.

They came up with the following: withholding; secretive; power struggles; dominant leaders; manipulations; game-playing; win–lose competition; sniping; prejudices; very little good contact between members; splitting within the team; highly political; no mutual respect; mismatches between what is said and what is acted on.

3   Finally Sue commented that people always have within them the capacity to
care and support each other. In fact that is their heart's deepest desire. She
then asked the team to identify as many issues as they could that lead people
away from a caring disposition to one that is uncaring and dispassionate.

Some of the comments that they came up with were: autocratic leadership;
blaming culture; hidden fears (they listed many); being shamed; intimidation;
unchallenged misassumptions about each other; humiliation; energy always
focused on the one good idea rather than a diversity of ideas; hidden conflict –
not dealt with; decisions get made outside meetings; meetings are all business
and no personal contact; hidden agendas; no shared values or purpose.

This exercise was very insightful in recognizing the different emotional dynamics
in the team and in exploring how they could change these dynamics to become
more productive and supportive of each other.

THE INVISIBILITY OF CONFORMITY

It is tasteless, odourless, invisible, passive and addictive. Like any drug, we take to
it as though we are indestructible. Conformity can kill.

Already organizations are dying because they did not realize the destructiveness of this 'drug'. Like the long-term effects of a drug, over-conforming cultures
lose their vitality and innovation, and people join together in a single colourless
mass. The drug slowly eats away at people's boundaries, at their self-identity, until
there is little left except ONE. You might think this is a bit extreme but just take a
look at yourself and those around you. How much of this drug have you and they
taken in? What is the impact? How much of you do you really bring into your workplace? Does the real you get left at home? Do you really know the people that you
work with?

SO WHAT CAN YOU DO?

We tend to think that isolation and clear boundaries are the best way to maintain individuality. But in the world of self-organizing structures, we learn that useful boundaries
develop through openness to the environment. (Wheatley 1992, p.93)

Openness

We hear people requesting openness at their workplace as though it can be turned
on and off at the flick of a switch. Yes, openness is critical for diversity, but people
will only be open if the conditions are right, if they feel safe to do so. Here we hit a
paradox because openness – that is, self-disclosure – is one of the ingredients for
securing a safe environment.

There is an answer, which emerges from the realization that in self-disclosure there are many layers, and there is choice:

- The top layer might simply reveal that you have a preference in the food that you eat.
- A deeper layer might reveal that you feel irritated by a colleague's lateness and you realize that you are measuring them against your own standards.
- An even deeper layer might reveal that you have a mole on your right buttock that is causing you concern.

What is appropriate? That is the question that you have to ask. Modelling appropriate self-disclosure, and encouraging others to do the same, will trigger the processes needed for building a safe environment – a place where people feel able to be open.

Being aware

Carrying an awareness that multiple realities exist (see Chapter 7), that 'my reality is different to yours', immediately impacts on your expectations in a way that supports diversity. It can lead you to investigate, invite exploratory dialogue and uncover the full meaning of events that offer opportunities to build on the hidden worlds of diversity around you.

Listening

This means listening to how things are from other people's viewpoints, without interpretation. Listening is about listening with all your senses.

Avoiding and preventing interpretation

Interpretation imposes your own truth on the situation by fitting other people's experience into your view of things; in so doing you could unwittingly close down and discount their experience and their reality. Avoiding interpretation can be quite difficult to do when shifting from a culture of conformity to one of diversity, especially when other people invite you to interpret. One way to respond to such an invitation is by simply stating your observations, or giving your viewpoint and making it clear that this is your interpretation, and that others may give a different interpretation.

Staying with the immediate experience

There is an element of comfort in relating present experiences to the past in order to make sense of them. Putting these to one side, parking your expectations and simply staying with the immediacy of the moment will enable you to discover a new world that is opening as you experience it. Without a blanket from the past the present becomes clearer, with an increasing possibility for connecting with others and valuing the full colour that they, and you, bring.

CONCLUSION

Discovering your difference can be like discovering yourself for the first time. It can be fun, daunting, mysterious, unnerving, unpredictable, strange, colourful, revealing, awakening. The meeting place is always at the boundary. Like the sea meeting the shore, this boundary has the potential for becoming a rich and fertile feeding ground. There are skills involved: uniting at the boundary does not come naturally to us much of the time, and there is plenty to learn. But the shoreline is not as pure as it may seem. There are hidden traps that we must be wary of: specu-lation, the push and pull of emotions, conflict, single-mindedness, the many layers in difference. Diversity for the individual is both a joy and a challenge.

REFERENCE

Wheatley, Margaret J. (1992), *Leadership and the New Science*, San Fransisco: Berrett-Koehler.

8 The courage to be different

INTRODUCTION

What does it take to be different? What animates an organization into really facing the challenge of its own diversity? What inspires leaders and managers to take the power of the potential around them and use it productively? What motivates an individual to be different; to bring themselves fully and openly into their work, rather than wither into a world of conformity?

It takes a willingness to face the fears that lock uniqueness in; the courage to take risks that unlock potential, and the ability to utilize support for opening the door into new ways of working.

FACING FEAR

What is it that blocks an organization from its diversity, from the potential that can offer such a rich source for success?

One answer to this question is fear:

- fear of ridicule;
- fear of making mistakes;
- fear of failure;
- fear of the unknown;
- fear of losing control;
- fear of becoming powerless and ineffective in a ruthless business world;
- fear of being overtaken by competitors, or even taken over by competitors.

Yet an organization is an abstract concept – it does not feel fear. It is the people in organizations that carry the fear – and fear is often imagined rather than a reality. This is not to say that fear is useless to mankind. Our ability to discriminate well is very important. Being discriminatory for self-protection and the protection of others is fine as long as judgement is skilful and based on rationale. Yet much of our fear is irrational. Fear is one of the greatest barriers to living and working in a world of diversity. When people are fearful of diversity they are afraid of bringing their own uniqueness into their lives and their work, and they fear the uniqueness of others.

WHAT DO PEOPLE FEAR ABOUT BEING DIFFERENT THEMSELVES?

isolation	ridicule
shame	blame
guilt	losing your power
making mistakes	revealing your vulnerability
rejection	losing your job or status
being successful	failing
rocking the boat	humiliation

No doubt you could add to this list, and we could take each one and challenge the reality of the perceptions behind them. But there is another way of looking at fear and being different – to be fearful usually involves other people. For example, to fear shame means to fear being shamed by another, or others; to fear rejection means to fear being rejected by others; to fear revealing your vulnerability means that you are afraid that others might hurt you if you are open; to fear isolation means to fear being separated from others. Your fear is simply a speculation of the future based on what you have seen, heard or experienced in the past. Many fears are irrational.

When an organization is fearful of bringing its diversity into the marketplace, then this is a result of the collective fear of the leaders in that organization. Such fears are often denied and covered up.

WHAT DO PEOPLE FEAR ABOUT OTHER PEOPLE'S DIFFERENCE?

Diversity is not just about your own fears about yourself and what may happen to you in revealing your spikes; you might also fear other people's spikes. Your ability to discriminate efficiently is put into question. Put another way, if everyone conforms to the same values, the same rules, the same patterns of behaviour, the same ways of working, it is easier to 'play the game'. People around you are predictable. You can make assumptions about how people will react, you can manipulate and be manipulated. You are less likely to find yourself in situations that you do not understand. You might not feel fulfilled but you feel relatively safe.

So what would happen if you worked in an environment where difference was valued? You would probably find yourself in situations where the only way to make sense of another person would be to ask questions, to show your ignorance or naïvety about the way they act and think.

What this reveals is fear of:

- unpredictability and loss of control;
- exposing your own ignorance or naïvety and having to ask questions;
- others being better than yourself;
- lack of understanding;
- other people's ideas being forced on to you (culminating in the 'not invented here syndrome');
- being 'shown up' by employees in lower positions.

So how can you manage fear? One way is to turn it on its head:

Turning fear on its head

Negative	Positive
Fear of losing control and facing unpredictability	Enjoying spontaneity, building on impulses, and the freedom to explore emerging ideas.
Feeling naïve and having to ask questions	Respecting your naïvety; arousing your curiosity to discover the tapestry and colour of the world. Recognizing opportunities to learn new knowledge and experiences.
Feeling intimidated by others who appear more creative and innovative than yourself	Valuing what others bring to the scene and drawing on their potential to complement yours.
Lack of understanding	Learning the art of asking questions and in so doing increasing your own knowledge base.
Other people's ideas being forced on to you (culminating in the 'not invented here' syndrome)	In a diversity culture both involvement and choice are important even when directives are made; it is the way in which they are made that makes a difference.
Being 'shown up' by employees in lower positions	Valuing and building on the rich resources available to you in the workplace wherever these resources exist. Recognizing the potential of your staff can be rewarding for both you and them.

Becoming aware of your own fears will make a difference; turning fearful imaginings into productive realities can be magical.

SELF-FULFILLING BEHAVIOUR

Fears and imaginings are often reinforced by behaviour that is 'self-fulfilling'. In these patterns of behaviour people manipulate their observations and experiences in a way that confirms rather than challenges their beliefs. Such behaviour keeps things the same rather than seeking change and acknowledging a different truth. Although self-fulfilling behaviour can be very positive and useful, here we look at self-fulfilling behaviours that are destructive to people's lives. It is an attribute of prejudice, and like a virus in a computer it can grow and spread. We see it here in the sad tale of Round and Square Blob.

A SAD BLOB STORY

Round Blob and Square Blob had been together for many years. They had three little Blobs – Blue Blob, Green Blob and Yellow Blob. Round and Square were finding life together increasingly difficult. Round tried to talk about it to Square but Square always had an excuse not to. Eventually they separated and went their own way. Round set up home nearby to be close to the little Blobs. But sadly things got worse. Square had a friend, Diamond, who told Square how awful Round was to leave the home in 'that way'. This made Square feel very angry towards Round.

On a number of occasions when Round called to see the little Blobs they were out, so Round stopped calling so much. Square concluded from this that Round no longer cared about them all. Round also concluded that Square and the little Blobs no longer cared. Both Square and Round got very angry and upset – they blamed each other for this state of affairs.

As time went on Square made many wrong assumptions about Round, as did Round about Square – they both acted as though these assumptions were true, only seeing those things that supported their beliefs. For example, Round saw a different-shaped car outside Square's house one Saturday night and immediately assumed that Square had found a new shape to live with. In fact the car belonged to cousin Splat who wanted somewhere to stay overnight. Poor Round did not sleep that night. Round's worst fears were confirmed – the break-up had been because Square loved someshape else. The next day Round decided to move farther away. Round could not bear to see Square and the little Blobs living with another shape. Round still loved them all very much, but on Sunday morning, with rucksack and dragging feet, Round slowly rolled down the long dusty track out of town.

At the same time Square had been talking to cousin Splat and realized that the shape who was most important to them all was Round. Square realized that many misassumptions had been made from distorted information, when all the time Square had been scared of losing everything that was important – Round and the little Blobs. Square had believed that this would happen because that is what happened to other shapes – and it started to happen when Round left home. The only way to keep the little Blobs had been to keep them away from Round. Square still loved Round very much and so did the little Blobs. Square ran down the road to Round's house only to find the 'For Sale' sign up and Round gone. Square was very sad and upset.

This, for now, is the end of the sad Blob story – or could it be the beginning of a happy Spiky story?

The truth is often painful, not because it confirms our beliefs but because it does not confirm them. In any situation there are many truths, but where there is a fixed way of behaving, as in self-fulfilling behaviours, there are fixed imaginings about what the truth is, or what the truth would bring. Lurking behind these imaginings is fear: fear of losing loved ones, or fear of losing power, status, belongings, credibility, and so on.

We need other people to help us see our fixed patterns of thinking and behaving, and to follow our heartfelt truths. People who collude with our situation are unhelpful; they just add fuel to the fire, as Diamond did in the story. They may make us feel good at the time because they 'appear' supportive, but they simply maintain the stuckness.

Facing up to the truth takes courage. It means opening up your heart to discover your own unique truth, from which your integrity can grow and flourish.

THE COURAGE TO TAKE RISKS

Courage   The power or quality of facing fear.
The confidence to act in accordance with one's beliefs. (*Collins English Dictionary*)

To create change we usually have to do something different – everything new that we do is an experiment. Therefore any new step is potentially dangerous, risky, uncertain, embarrassing. Totally being yourself, bringing your difference fully into life, means facing fear and finding the confidence to act in accordance with your beliefs. The courage to speak your truth.

The courage to overcome fear means:

● taking action in the face of that fear.

The courage to experiment means:

● facing the likelihood of not getting it right the first time. It also means trying different experiments and being creative with a range of possibilities.

The courage to speak out means:

- risking rocking the boat and finding the courage to face instability;
- taking a risk to evoke change and finding the courage to stay with uncertainty;
- taking the risk of being innovative and finding the courage to take responsibility for your suggestions;
- risking exposure and finding the courage to feel vulnerable.

To en-courage is to support others in finding the courage that they need to truly be themselves at work, and in their lives.

DIVERSITY SUPPORT

Finding courage and taking risks is easier if you feel well supported. Additional support is required when stepping into the unknown – for yourself and everyone else who is seeking the courage to be different.

The concept of support in organizations is, in the main, widely misunderstood. It is often prejudiced as the 'soft' side of people skills. This prejudice often comes from people who do not have an adequate sense of self-awareness and therefore neither support themselves well nor know how to support others well.

People often have a fixed idea of the meaning of support: for instance, hugs for women when they are in tears; telling the team what they have to do when they are not achieving the results that you would like; colluding with the situation (as Diamond did in the Blob story); doing the work for them when they do not appear to be managing it themselves. Of course these responses may be appropriate in certain circumstances, but when it is perceived that this is the full extent of support it is not surprising that prejudice arises.

The most common mistake that people make when they offer support is to transfer their own needs or feelings on to the other person, like projecting an image on to a screen. They then act as though what they now perceive is true of the other person. You might do this in two different ways:

1 You give the type of support to the other person that you would want for yourself if you were in that same predicament.

   For example, a member of your team arrives at work in casual clothes, which is not the norm. He is receiving some criticism from the rest of the team so you suggest that he takes the time to go home and change – rather than invite the team to change the norms.

   What you assume to be needed by the other person may be the very thing that locks the situation into a cycle which sustains the predicament, rather than encourages change.

2 You transfer your own discomforts and emotions on to the other person and assume these emotions to be true for them.

For example, a female colleague takes a risk in a very important management meeting by suggesting that the business strategy which management have spent the last six weeks developing will not work. As a member of the management team you feel nervous at being challenged or even exposed in this way. Rather than owning these discomforts you attribute them to your colleague as though she is the one who is feeling challenged and exposed – you give her the support that you think she needs to untangle the mess you perceive her to be in (added to this you are likely to make sure that she does not expose your vulnerability again).

What a sad state this is, but one that many would secretly recognize.

BUILDING SUPPORT

There are three interlinked dimensions to support that you can pay attention to when developing a culture that respects and values diversity (Figure 8.1).

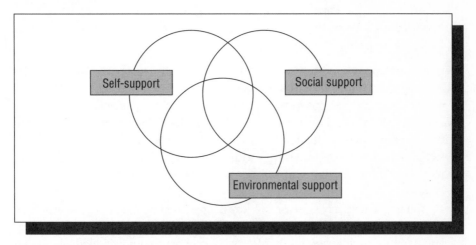

Figure 8.1   Interlinked dimensions of support

1 **Self-support** is how you and others take care of yourselves physically, mentally and emotionally in bringing difference into the workplace. In order to do this well you need to develop a good sense of self-awareness. Self-awareness enables you to recognize your needs and then to seek the appropriate support to meet these needs. If you lack self-support then either you act unsupported, or others will misread the support that they think you need. Your support system becomes dysfunctional.

Self-awareness also widens your scope for choice. When you identify your needs and recognize the support that you require to stretch the limits of your boundaries – to show your spikes – then you have choice. Your first choice is where you position yourself in that situation, at that time, on the conformity–diversity continuum (Figure 8.2).

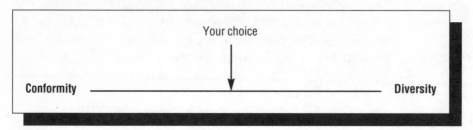

Figure 8.2   The conformity–diversity continuum

To start with you might choose to be a conformist and wait to see what other people do, or you might choose to take a first step along the continuum towards diversity. Paradoxically, as soon as you begin to make choices you begin to move, because the choice is coming from your unique self rather than being part of a collective habitual response.

2   **Social support** is both the individual and collective support which is in the large system; the culture of the organization. For example, a blaming culture would not be very supportive. A culture that supports learning and therefore supports experimentation would be. When taking risks you need to be able to trust that others will not attack your vulnerability, because bringing your diversity into the workplace also brings with it your vulnerability. So you will need to feel safe and know that you will not be attacked or humiliated by your colleagues.

You might also have one or two key people you can turn to in the organization who you know will give you the sort of support that you most need, when you need it. Equally you might offer your support to other individuals as and when they need it.

3   **Environmental support** is the physical support within the immediate and surrounding environment of the organization: the layout of the furniture, the position of the building, the presence or absence of pollutants in the environment, where you are positioned to work, availability of resources, and so on. In a diverse culture you would expect to find some flexibility in these areas.

Homeworking, where both men and women are increasingly able to choose to work from home, is an example of environmental support, because it supports their need for a balance between work and home life.

THE COURAGE OF AN ORGANIZATION

It is not too difficult to look around and see the courage of some leaders and organizations who have taken bold steps – leaders who have brought their individuality into the open, modelling good practice for their employees to do the same:

- **Anita Roddick, The Body Shop** – who has shown us the courage of a woman who brought soul into the world of business and humanity into the workplace.
- **Richard Branson, The Virgin Empire** – who regularly brings his integrity and unique self to the forefront of his business empire.
- **Ricardo Semler, Semco** – who challenged his workforce to bring their unique selves into the workplace and in so doing discovered a collective potential they had not foreseen.

These people are not without their critics, but then such success never is and indeed criticism is to be acknowledged and valued. In good criticism there is energy and diversity, people seeing things from a different perspective and a different viewpoint. Such criticism can offer invaluable building blocks for future initiatives.

So does this mean that diversity is dependent on leaders taking the first steps? Or do these leaders separate themselves from employees along the conformity–diversity continuum?

CREATING A COURAGEOUS CULTURE

In the case of Ricardo Semler, no. His mission is to draw on the potential of his workforce, and he can only do this by valuing their uniqueness and encouraging employees to speak out. It has meant working with different paradigms from the ones industry has come to believe are the most efficient and effective for business success. Repetitive work on production lines is replaced by 'manufacturing cells' where small groups of people work with a product from beginning to end. There are costs, but the benefits outweigh the costs – especially when human satisfaction is brought into the equation.

Semler writes:

> We simply do not believe our employees have an interest in coming in late, leaving early and doing as little as possible for as much money as their union can wheedle out of us. After all these same people raise children, join the PTA, elect mayors, governors, senators and presidents. They are adults. At Semco we treat them as adults. We trust them. (Semler 1993, p. 58)

In Semco:

- Ricardo Semler does not expect employees to do that which he cannot do, or does not practise himself.
- Innovation is regarded as the norm, not a special occasion to be rewarded with prizes.
- The philosophy of Semco is built on participation and involvement. Employees are encouraged to speak out, give their opinions, to say what they think – and they are listened to.
- Strikes are considered to be normal as long as the strikes represent what the people of the company think and feel.
- People wear what they want to wear, appearance is not a factor in hiring and promoting people.
- Employees are free to adapt, change and even decorate their working areas as they please, to suit themselves and the people working around them.

'Semco is one of Latin-America's fastest growing companies, acknowledged to be the best in Brazil to work for and with a waiting list of thousands of applicants hoping to join.' (Semler 1993, back cover)

It seems that it is easier for employees to be courageous when their leader recognizes that the potential of the business is in the diversity of the workforce. The support that such a leader brings to the organization is immense, simply because they recognize and respect each individual for their unique self. Ricardo Semler is a leader who succeeds through releasing control as opposed to holding on to it.

CONCLUSION

Being different means being courageous. In courage there is fear, often irrational and imagined fear rather than a truth. To take courage and face our fears we need support. That support often begins with the courage of leaders, but ultimately it must permeate through to the very heart of the organization if the courage of the many is to be brought to the surface. Without the right support you and your fellow workers will not face your fears, nor take the courage that can truly make a difference to yourselves and to the business.

REFERENCE

Semler, Ricardo (1993), *Maverick*, London: Arrow.

9   Standing up and standing out

INTRODUCTION

This whole subject of diversity is riddled with paradox. Every time that it seems we have found a way to explore how energizing and creative diversity can be, up pops another paradox for us to pay attention to.

As the authors of this book, it fascinates us to see how, when diversity is encouraged and people and organizations stand up and stand out, they are punished for doing so. This is so common that it is not surprising that most people want to hide their spikes and 'stay hidden'.

WHY PEOPLE SEEK TO PUNISH DIFFERENCE

Being different means questioning the basis of how others behave, or implying that they too should be different. This can lead to others feeling threatened, devalued or belittled in some way. When this happens people tend to react defensively and one form of defence is attack. So people are attacked and punished for being different.

Such punishment can be clear, for example sending people to Coventry, or ridiculing them. Other forms of punishment are more subtle, where people are passed over for promotion, do not get the chance to join the management development programme, or are not invited to the ball, and so on. The whole purpose of the punishment is to bring these people 'back into line'.

When organizations stand up and stand out they can find that they lose customers, or receive unpleasant media attention questioning the basis of their difference. As a result the organization's public image and share price might suffer. When organizations compete in the marketplace the tendency is for them to become more like their competitors rather than unlike them, as if each has to be better at what the other is doing instead of doing something different. The reason for this seems to be that fickle customers may well punish them for being different by staying with what they know and are comfortable with. Paradoxically, it is those organizations that have taken the risk to be different that have eventually prospered.

BUILDING A FEAR OF DIFFERENCE INTO OUR CULTURE

There are four powerful factors that help to build a fear of being different at all the levels of large systems, small systems and individuals. These are:

- To survive people have to belong.
- Friendship is based on confluence.
- Control and order are based on deference and conformity.
- Security comes from fitting in.

TO SURVIVE PEOPLE HAVE TO BELONG

As we have said in Chapter 7, the need to belong is a fundamental part of our birth, growth and development. As we start life our very survival depends upon how well we learn to conform. As children grow older they start to explore their spikes. Finding the balance between individuality and belonging is the very stuff of survival and it becomes deeply ingrained in each of us.

Of course these early experiences differ enormously for different people in terms of the extent to which the balance between individuality and belonging is reached. For some there is little opportunity for individuality, for others the scope is considerable. Regardless of the level we reach, each of us finds the best way to survive in the particular circumstance in which we find ourselves.

So the first and earliest lesson is that if we wish to belong and survive we have to conform with the family culture. To do otherwise threatens us with expulsion and, at a basic level, with death.

FRIENDSHIP IS BASED ON CONFLUENCE

As people grow and move outside the confines of the family and make contact with other young people they soon receive messages about fitting in and being 'good' rather than standing out and being 'naughty'. Children who are 'well behaved' – that is, who fit the norms of the controlling adults – are rewarded. Children who are naughty – who question the norms – are punished. Young people also begin to notice that making friends means finding other children who like the things they like and behave in a similar way.

It is quite unusual for 'well-behaved' children to make friends with 'naughty' children. The 'good' children may admire the 'bad' children's daring, but also probably think they are silly for standing out and being punished. Naughty children have a tendency to make friends with other naughty children.

So friendship in our early years is based largely on being confluent with our friends and fitting in with the observed standards of behaviour. This is demonstrated when young people form groups and have particular patterns of behaviour that have to be conformed with if they want to be members of the group or gang. Even when young people want to be different they tend to want to find others who will be different with them, e.g. punks and gothics. If we are different in an individual way we may also be friendless and alone.

CONTROL AND ORDER ARE BASED ON DEFERENCE AND CONFORMITY

School has a major impact on our need to defer to and conform with the rules imposed by adults. It is normal in most schools for young people to be grouped in classes by age and sometimes by ability. This grouping of like ages and like abilities is constraining, limiting and uncreative. If people are all alike who are they going to learn from? The answer of course is the teacher, the adult. This removes the possibility of peer learning where younger children learn from older children and from each other and do so in a supportive and cooperative way. What happens is that children learn from knowledgeable adults in a competitive environment.

In order for this system to work young people have to be controlled and disciplined and are expected to defer to the wishes of the teacher. Young people are also expected to wear uniforms so that they even look alike.

The rules about being 'well behaved' continue and are reinforced by all kinds of rewards and punishments. Young people also meet the concept of being tested. Not only are they expected to learn in a stilted and rigid way, but also to be examined on how well they are doing the learning. Getting good grades becomes a driving force that demands deference and conformity to the learning process. Freedom is restricted and the ethic of 'hard work' is introduced at a time when growing people should be having fun.

What people learn in this stage of their development is that if they behave, work hard and get good grades then they will do well in their lives. In this context 'doing well' is synonymous with getting a job. And surprise, surprise, when young people do get a job they discover that the need for deference and conformity continues. The rules may be different and the forms of punishment and reward more subtle, but really nothing changes – it just seems more adult.

So we all learn that to get on we need to defer and conform, and not to do so risks being forced to leave. A scary and threatening scenario, to be sure.

SECURITY COMES FROM FITTING IN

One of the basic needs people have is to feel secure – to know they have and will continue to have food, water, shelter, clothing and clean air to breathe, and to love and be loved. Many people, perhaps the majority, do not have such security and so life is a constant and continuing state of anxiety.

To avoid such insecurity people learn that they need to fit in with the norms of the society in which they live. After all, they have had a lifetime's training in doing just that. By fitting in they may be able to gain some modicum of security for themselves and their families. To stand out and run against the crowd instead of with it, is to risk one's security.

> Trevor Bentley recalls leaving his high-paid executive job to become a freelance consultant. In his own words, 'I had to climb out of the fur-lined rut and sacrifice my security for the freedom of the open road'.
>
> He has learned to live without the security of a full-time job and has settled instead for, again in his own words, 'the real security that only freedom from deference and conformity can bring'.

But for many people choosing to make a stand for individual freedom in this way is too risky. The very real fear and anxiety of not being able to meet their basic needs stops them. It is no wonder that when, after many years of service, people are made redundant they are bereft, depressed and unable to adjust. And then they fit into the masses of the unemployed and disappear yet again.

The fear of difference is so well instilled into most people that it is seen as threatening and something to be avoided. This in turn leads to people holding strong prejudices and unfairly discriminating against those who appear different and behave differently from them. The process begins with stereotyping.

STEREOTYPING

Stereotyping is a healthy and useful process because it creates stability. It means that every time we go out of the door in the morning we do not have to go through a lengthy process of making sense of the world from the beginning. We can build on past information, knowledge and experiences. The trouble is we get lazy, we rely too much on our ability to do this and consequently do not spend enough time checking out the assumptions that exist within established stereotypes – we allow these assumptions to travel too deeply without question into our understanding of the world. This leads to a fixation of our view of the world (Figure 9.1).

Checking your stereotypes means becoming aware of the assumptions that you make about people and situations, and continuously updating your repertoire of knowledge.

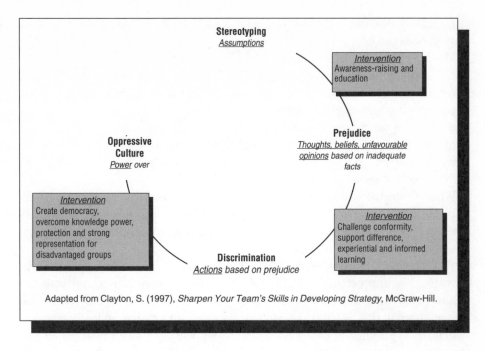

Figure 9.1 The process that leads to destructive discrimination

PREJUDICE AND DISCRIMINATION

Prejudice generally means holding fixed beliefs which push us into behaving so that we treat other people in an unfavourable way. In other words we don't treat them in a way in which they have a right to be treated, that is, as we would want to be treated ourselves or as they would like to be treated.

It is no surprise therefore that most people tend to deny that they are prejudiced in any way, and yet we all are. We cannot avoid being prejudiced in some way or other. In fact having prejudices is one of the reasons that we survive in a largely hostile world. We base many of our choices on our underlying prejudices and we do this unaware that we are doing so.

For example, for many years Trevor has had a deep prejudice against child abusers, something that he could readily rationalize. It was not until he discovered that he had been abused himself as a child that he understood the basis of his prejudice.

As we grow up we are given many messages from parents and teachers that condition our understanding of the world. Most of these are valuable and helpful but others are prejudices that people in authority pass on to us as being truths. Our choices have been coloured by these prejudices and it is not until we recognize that we have prejudices that we can start to make more informed choices about how we want to behave.

Making choices in an aware way is what we mean by being discriminating. Yet the expression 'discrimination' has come to have the unpleasant connotation of behaving out of prejudice rather than choice. There is muddle and confusion about what it means to discriminate.

On the one hand, when we discriminate we are making a carefully thought out choice of fine distinction between alternative actions or things. On the other hand, when we discriminate we are acting on prejudice in a conditioned response to some person or event.

When people deny their prejudices it leads them to act in an unthinking conditioned way that is not in any way discriminating, but which is described as discrimination. It is no wonder then that there is confusion and uncertainty about the whole concept of discrimination.

When people's prejudices are built into an organization's culture, again in an unaware way, the people in the organization, who respond in accord with the culture, do so in a way that reinforces the prejudices. When prejudices become systematized in this way the system then becomes oppressive, and oppression in turn leads to unthinking conditioned conformity where differences are seen as a threat.

DISCRIMINATION AND QUALITY

If we turn our attention to discrimination as the exercise of fine judgement and choice we can see that to be highly discriminating is the only way that we can achieve high quality of products and services. To be highly discriminating does in turn mean being highly attuned to difference and to operating in a highly differentiated way.

The whole approach to quality, particularly initiatives such as Total Quality Management, is towards creating a widespread attitude of being discriminating in everything that people do. This cannot be achieved in an atmosphere of conformity, although it would seem that 'conforming' to standards is what we are aiming for. To the contrary, what really matters is that people are encouraged to differentiate and discriminate so that the very best practices are able to flourish.

Here is an example of what we mean:

A particular product, a circular cutting disc for a coal-mining machine, required a circular flange to be cut from a sheet of steel. This was the standard to which people conformed. An apprentice engineer working in the factory attended an in-house seminar on cost control and cost reduction which was intended to encourage people to reduce wastage wherever possible. The apprentice engineer, who was working on cutting the circular flanges, saw the extent of the waste created and suggested it could be reduced if the flange was cut in three segments and welded together, and he argued it would be stronger. The idea was tried out and the test showed it to be very successful, making a significant cost saving and increasing quality. As a result of this many other aspects of work were re-examined and people were encouraged to differentiate and discriminate in all aspects of their work.

BREAKING THROUGH AND SHOWING OUR SPIKES

If you can imagine the cloying need to conform as a tough sheet of cling film covering your spiky individuality, then as you start to push towards the boundary of your difference the spikes press on the cling film until finally they break through.

What a sense of relief and release comes with this breaking out. Once it has happened there is no going back: conforming becomes a choice, being different becomes a choice and living fully becomes a choice. The excitement that accompanies this breaking through is breathtaking.

A group of people who work together as a management team had been struggling with the growth of their organization. The creativity they needed was present but was not being offered. As individual managers and as a team they were stuck. They described this as 'not rocking the boat'. No one wanted to capsize the boat, but as the boat was stuck on a sandbank it needed rocking to shift it. After working together over a development weekend where they were encouraged to show their spikes and to rock the boat, they have forged ahead.

CONCLUSION

There is a risk in breaking through for individuals, teams and organizations, but the benefits are quite simply enormous. We are all so much more than we ever dare to be. Our fear is deeply ingrained and not easily faced. Yet when it is, it is like the sun breaking through a cloudy sky.

10   The power of potential

Potent-ial	being or becoming but not yet in existence;
	possible but not yet actual;
	latent but unrealized ability or capacity.
Potent	possessing great strength; powerful. (*Collins English Dictionary*)

INTRODUCTION

In diversity there is potential, both collectively and individually. Potential is a powerful force towards personal fulfilment and organizational achievements. We cannot ignore it and it is something that few of us understand well. The crucial question seems to be, how can we align the potential of the individual with the potential of the business?

1 We can only realize full potential through diversity – not through confluence. Potential is bounded by our actions as much as it is released by our actions.
2 We cannot determine the potential of a business separately from the collective potential of the workforce. The potential of a business *is* its workforce.
3 The fulfilment of the business potential is affected by the local and world economy, by the growth potential of the industry and by the way the organization responds to these external influences.
4 We tend to talk about potential as though it is a fixed entity. In the authors' experience that is not the case: potential is fluid, moving, evolving, growthful, and often mysterious. Furthermore we have many different potentials in both *what* we are capable of doing and achieving, as well as *how* we do what we do.

There are three important principles that we must know about and trust, that will lead us towards releasing potential in the workplace (Figure 10.1).

The knowledge and wisdom contained in these three principles underpin our work.

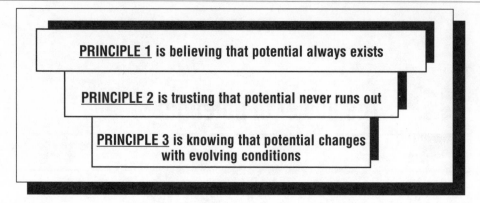

Figure 10.1   Three principles for releasing potential

BOUNDED POTENTIAL

Potential is bounded by our actions as much as it is released by our actions.

If the organization is predominantly conforming, with working conditions based on narrowly defined parameters, then it will be difficult to draw on the potential that exists. Conversely, in organizations where diversity is encouraged and working parameters have scope and flexibility, potential will simply emerge and grow.

TWO PLUS ONE MAKES MORE THAN THREE

The basic ingredients of potential are two plus one. Two people plus an attractor in the environment:

The story of Sue's daughter, a friend and a bouncy ball

When my daughter was a little girl I bought her a small bouncy ball. You have probably seen them: the harder you bounce the ball the higher it bounces, then if you don't catch it, it will bounce all over the place and for a while cause much amusement.

Eventually the ball fell to the bottom of the toy box and was forgotten until many months later when we had the 'annual toy box sort-out'. Out came the bouncy ball again, this time with a friend around. To start with, my daughter and her friend bounced the ball to see how high it would go; they built sand-castles and a helter-skelter, rolling the ball down the spiral; the ball became a visitor to an imaginary toy town made of twigs from the garden; the two friends then used it to play with water and roll it around to make patterns in paint. Over the following days they came up with many more ideas to play with this little bouncy ball.

The play potential of the children was being *realized* through their imagination with the ball, and *released* in play. The only limitation of the ball was in its physical structure; there appeared to be no limitations to the ideas. What was particularly noticeable was that the potential for the ball increased as the diversity of these two children came into 'play', as their potential emerged. My daughter appeared to be the one with vision: she would create the imaginary town, whereas her friend was much more action oriented, bringing the town to life with imaginary people and animals. It seemed that their games with the ball would not have happened if they had been playing alone. The potential of the ball was only achieved through the release of the play potential of these two children. The only limitation here was the imagination of the children – and that did not seem very limiting, given the flexibility that I generally encouraged in the home.

THE BOUNDARIES TO POTENTIAL

There are four apparent boundaries in the story that impact in different ways on potential, and which can be translated into organizations:

1   The context in which the children were playing – the home.
    This is equivalent to the culture of an organization and the small systems in which people work. In other words what freedoms or constraints exist in the culture and environment?
2   The physical structure of the ball.
    Equivalent to the freedoms or constraints that exist with the material or technical aspects of products and services.
3   The collective imagination of the two children.
    Equivalent to the limits of the diversity that exists in a team or an organization. The freedoms and constraints of what exists, or does not exist in the differences between people.
4   The respect of the two children for each other and for their different contribution to their play constructs.
    Equivalent to valuing diversity and engaging with difference in the workplace – the freedoms and constraints of relationships.

There is no doubt that if Sue's relationship with her daughter had been bounded by conformity, or freedom to play had been limited by strict boundaries, then the children's play would have reflected this. Their potential was bounded by Sue's control (and behaviour towards her daughter and the children); releasing potential means releasing these controls enough to achieve fulfilment. Conformity often arises in childhood when children get rewarded for doing as they are told, and punished, often shamed, for experimenting and taking bold steps – that is, both inside and outside the home.

Had the latter been the case, instead of producing her own ideas Sue's daughter would simply have gone along with the solitary ideas of her friend, or have been looking to Sue for suggestions. She would have been checking with Sue to see if it was okay to take certain actions. Their play would most certainly have been different – playing with the ball would probably have been short lived.

Earlier we mentioned that the basic ingredients of potential are two plus one. Two people plus an attractor in the environment. The attractor (a person, an object, a situation, an event, a project, and so on) is whatever a person is drawn towards as a means of releasing their potential. In the workplace this could range from a chosen profession, to leading or chairing a team meeting. The attractor *always* presents some level of challenge for you when it offers an opportunity for you to realize your potential in a particular way.

Why is it not one plus one? The authors believe it is less likely that an individual person can achieve their full potential on their own. We might set out to achieve our potential on our own at times, but it is never in isolation. Two plus one is the absolute minimum, the basic ingredients, the starting point. The ideal ingredients are often much more complex.

THE POTENTIAL OF A BUSINESS *IS* ITS WORKFORCE

'I really feel we have worked well as a team when we complete our work and I know I couldn't have done it on my own,' said the team member to his colleagues.

The purpose of working in groups and teams in a business is not just to make it easier for leaders and managers to manage large numbers of employees, but more so to achieve a greater potential than each individual could have achieved on their own. What often happens is that teams are seen as a structure to maintain control, rather than a means of increasing the potential of the business. Teams often deny themselves the power of their collective potential – at all levels in the organization.

In diversity there is potential.
In potential there is power.
In power there is often fear.

PEOPLE POWER

There is one fundamental principle that we must now acknowledge – potential carries power. This is different from empowerment as it is commonly understood. In many cases empowerment is narrowed down to the act of giving more people more responsibility. In view of this the use of the term 'empowerment' often attracts very mixed reactions, suggesting that the latent power in most organizations remains untapped. 'Giving' employees responsibility can be a very clever way of *not* addressing the power of people that exists in the system: the power in potential. It may be that people are afraid of releasing latent power for themselves and for others: 'If we take the lid off will we have anarchy? Will we find a can of worms that we/I cannot handle? Will I discover that I don't have the personal power to match the power bestowed on me by my status?' These questions convey fears and fears are frequently based on misperceptions and imaginings rather than realities.

We all know that certain types of power can be destructive, which can lead us to be fearful of it. Yet there is, of course, both positive and negative power. The power in potential is positive. It is the destructiveness in power which is misdirected, that turns the power in potential into negative power. Fear is often central to negative power. Fear will lead people to act 'in pretence' of organizational values and manipulate words and concepts so that they make meaning in a way that avoids confrontation or exposure of their fear. For those who fear the most, the skill of manipulation is an art form.

The predicament is that as long as leaders and managers fear their power and the power in their employees, the concept of power remains negative rather than positive. Tapping into the collective potential of the organization becomes inhibited.

THE PATH OF LEAST RESISTANCE

There are a few caring organizations where it is possible to talk freely of fears and concerns. In these organizations anxiety diminishes as fears and concerns are addressed. On the other hand there are many hostile working environments where it is truly unsafe for people to reveal their fears and concerns. In these organizations anxiety increases when fear is suppressed, as much as when it is exposed.

This poses quite a dilemma – what does one do?

An impulsive response is to encourage openness, as though openness can occur at the flick of a switch. But to be open means to expose some aspects of your vulnerability – and people get hurt if they expose their vulnerability in hostile environments. Openness requires loving and caring from others. Yet these are words and attitudes that are rarely associated with the harsh business environments that many people work in. Asking for openness without asking for loving and caring as well can be a potentially painful request for those involved.

It may be that organizations of the future will build supportive communities where people feel cared for enough to be open about their fears and concerns. For now we must accept that these working environments are few and far between.

Meanwhile the question that confronts us is, 'How do we deal with fear when the environment is hostile?'

In diversity there is always choice, and so too you have choice in managing fears without having to probe deeply into them if this is inappropriate. The main skill is in making the process visible – not pretending that fear does not exist. Here are some more pointers:

- Clarify the issues being addressed.
- Appreciate and respect that where there are difficult issues being addressed, there are concerns and fears just beneath the surface.
- Look at the predicament from different perspectives, different angles, even turning it on its head.
- Recognize what you as an individual and/or as a team contribute to the problem.
- Connect with others and begin to recognize their different realities.
- Describe observations through metaphor.
- Turn negatives into positives.
- Ask others how the predicament might be resolved.
- Do nothing.
- Change why questions into what, how, where, when and whom questions.
- ....(add your own).

These interventions work best when everyone is valued for their contribution – *you* can show that you care, which may in turn lead to others becoming more caring.

THE IMPACT ON ORGANIZATIONAL POTENTIAL FROM EXTERNAL INFLUENCES

The fulfilment of your business potential will be affected by the local and world economy, by the growth potential of the industry, by competition and by the way your organization responds to these external influences. For instance, the growth of information technology (IT) in the last decade has tapped into the amazing potential of organizations and of individuals, for example Bill Gates of Microsoft. The potential that exists in computer technology and the arrival of the Internet has opened doors that even a decade ago were unheard of.

COMPETITION AND THE LOCAL AND WORLD ECONOMY

Changes in the local and world economy will also impact on a business and therefore on both the collective and individual potential in that organization. In a rising economic climate people become energized and potential is easily accessible, whereas in a declining economic climate energy can become depressed and potential appears to become less accessible. These are things that we cannot change, we can only change the way that we respond to them. If the local economy becomes depressed then it is easy for a business to be drawn into that depression. It is easy to forget that potential always exists, that it never runs out, and that potential changes with changing conditions.

Looking inward to the people in the organization, the diversity of ideas and views that can re-energize or redirect a business exists in its collective workforce:

> An example that we can draw on is that of Apple Computers, who virtually created the personal computer market, spawned the use of the spreadsheet and then developed the Macintosh graphic user interface. They were only eclipsed from a prime position by the might of IBM and its subsequent clones. When Steve Jobs and Steve Wozniac left Apple, the potential of the organization seemed to stall, despite many attempts and developments to maintain its major niche position. Jobs went on to develop the NeXT Company with its similar ability to release the potential of its workforce. Now that NeXT has been bought up by Apple and Jobs is back in the fold, it will be interesting to see if Apple can regain the ability to release the power of the corporate potential.

Clearly the potential within an organization is where its success will arise from. Releasing that potential in the face of tough competition in the industry and the changing local and world economy is the task of the leaders.

THE FLUIDITY OF POTENTIAL

THE MAGIC PURSE

> Potential is like a magic purse – the more you spend the more there is to be discovered.

Potential is not a fixed entity but a changing, fluid, ever-present resource for an organization, a resource that never runs out. But, like the magic purse, if you don't realize your potential, then potential exists only as potential, it does not change.

CHANGING POTENTIAL IN CHANGING CONDITIONS

Potential is most productive when linked to social, cultural, business and organizational needs and when it is satisfying for the person or people whose potential is being fulfilled. The conditions are constantly changing and evolving. The idea of a waterfall illustrates this point:

The potential of a waterfall is different at the peak of the rainy season compared to the peak of the dry season. In the rainy season it has the potential for generating electricity, in the dry season it has the potential for exploration of caves normally inaccessible during the rainy season. Over the years the shape and character of the waterfall will evolve, as will the wildlife in it.

The potential of the waterfall changes in accordance with social needs *and* evolution. Before electricity arrived, the potential of a waterfall or river would have been different, for instance to drive a water-wheel for grinding cereals.

People are very similar: how our potential is realized changes in accordance with evolution and social needs. Children's potential to absorb and understand computers – which is frequently far beyond the capabilities of many adults – was non-existent fifty years ago. The potential of athletes and sports celebrities to break records (without the use of drugs) is never ceasing – again, achievements that were unimaginable fifty years ago.

Equally a person will realize their potential in different ways in different organizations and in different roles, through what they do *and* how they do it.

UNLOCKING HIDDEN TALENTS

Talents are innate or natural abilities and aptitudes that are above average in a person's capabilities. Tucked away in the dark dusky corners of our lives are hidden talents, some realized in our earlier years and stored away in cupboards, lofts and boxes, others not yet discovered. When people bring their hidden talents out into the open the capabilities and skills that emerge can be awesome. People's hidden talents are often a mystery to us; that is part of their beauty. Some hidden talents are of little direct use in the workplace, but others can be, depending on how well matched the talent and the business are – for example taxi drivers with exceptional memory skills, or the ability to absorb and retain factual information.

Hidden talents tell us about people, about their diversity. The novelty of hidden talents can be a source of energy and vitality, as well as channels for making connections, for conversations and building friendships. The path of any relationship is unpredictable, yet the simple fact that new relationships happen increases the potential of a workforce. When people are allowed to bring their talents into the workplace, or when new talents are discovered, people connect.

If you begin today, and for the rest of your life assume that everyone you meet has at least one hidden talent, what a fascinating world you could encounter. You could start with identifying your own.

Finding your talent

Most of us have talents which we do not realize we have until we test them out. Yet we frequently do not test them out because we hold a belief that we are 'no good' – at drawing, writing, painting, playing music, growing plants, cooking, languages, design, memory, magic, sports, teaching, and so on.

The first thing that you could do is ask all the people you meet over the next week what talents they have. From this you can compile a list. You can also enquire about people's talents – how people have developed them, how long they have had them, could they show you the outcomes of their endeavours, and so on.

Add to your list any talents that you know you have, and any that interest you that are not on the list and which you have not developed in yourself. Then go down through your list and tick those that inspire you.

Taking the view that talents are fulfilling when we develop them, which of these talents do you now wish to pursue? Some people find their pursuits life-changing, like the fifty-year-old man who decided to learn to play a guitar and sing – he now performs in a rock group. Others have simply found that the novelty of new-found talents brings fresh energy and vitality into their lives.

CONCLUSION

Perhaps this is the chapter for drawing your own conclusions about you and your organization, by asking these two questions:

- Is your organization achieving its full potential?
- Are you and your team achieving your full potential?

If your answers are 'no', then there is no time to begin like the present.

11 Living and working at the edge

INTRODUCTION

Living and working at the edge of our potential is both risky and powerful. When people live and work at their outer edges they are able to exercise their personal power. This use of personal power is at the heart of discovering what passes for 'appropriate diversity' in any given situation.

The spiky diagram we have already introduced you to (see Figure 3.2) represents an explosion of personal energy, with the spikes being the outer reaches of the energy which is where we believe real contact is made with people and the environment and where people 'perform to their limits'. If the energy or power is contained by social and organizational norms (culture) the energy is not available for people to access and use when they perform.

Because we are all different we will present different shapes to the world. Our energy and power will flow differently and our experiences, interests and desires will be different. Our power will be experienced as being different, being unique to us.

OUR POWER IS OUR DIFFERENCE

Personal power is mostly exercised from a stance of being different, or at the edges of our spikiness.

Personal power is associated with confidence and self-esteem and enables people to make choices and decisions about their own lives in a way that ensures they live as they want to. People with a strong sense of personal power are able to listen to the ideas and suggestions of other people, to weigh up the advice they receive, and then act to suit themselves without being unduly swayed in the direction others might want them to be.

Personal power is centred on our difference, on our individuality and on our confidence to be fully and unashamedly ourselves. Being comfortable with who we are is a source of great personal power, so much so that some people are unnerved by people who exude self-belief and self-confidence.

Personal power should not be confused with role power. Role power is the power people have because of the role they happen to have at the time. It is possible to have several roles each of which carries a certain power. For example, you could be a father or mother, a manager, a husband or wife, captain of the hockey team, and so on. In each of these roles there is a certain designated, or assumed, power. This might be specified by the organization for whom we play the role, or implied from our experience or the expectations of others.

Both personal power and role power have to be recognized as quite different from reflected power, which is a level of power exercised by those close to 'powerful' people. They bask in the power that emanates from their more powerful companions. Personal assistants often operate with the reflected role power of their bosses. Children can express the reflected power of their parents – being the son of a prime minister, for example, can carry with it a lot of reflected power. Husbands and wives often operate with the reflected power of their partners.

This reflected power is often mistaken as the personal or role power of the individuals themselves rather than the person they are close to. The problem with this is the loss of sight as to whose power is being exercised. Recognizing and using reflected power is a valuable attribute and it needs full awareness of what they are doing on the part of the people using the reflected power.

In exercising power we all operate with a combination of personal power and role power and sometimes reflected power. The extent to which we are able to fully utilize our power depends on many factors including our upbringing, education, training, experience, the role we have, the people around us, and so on. Perhaps the most vital ingredient is the extent to which we are prepared to stand up and live and work at our growing edge.

OUR SPIKES ARE WHO WE ARE

When people make an impression on each other it is their spikes that make the impression. It is each other's differences that they notice and remember. When people hide their differences they merge into the background and disappear into the crowd. This is a very useful strategy to be able to choose when it is appropriate. However, if people want to make an impression, have influence and express themselves fully then it is through their differences that they do so.

People relate to each other and identify with each other by their spikes, and yet they are more than just their spikes. By showing their spikiness they let people know what to expect from them and so they do not take them by surprise. When people are open about their differences and when they show themselves fully, what people see at first is their external spikiness. People's differences show on the surface. Our gender, race, appearance and dress are the first spikes that people see. Later, as they get to know us better, they start to discover other spikes to do with our behaviour, then later still our beliefs and values. So gradually people discover the fullness of other people's spikiness and in the process they choose whether or not to continue the relationship.

WHEN PEOPLE MEET

When people meet for the first time a fascinating four-part process automatically switches on. This is a highly complex process that we have each developed in a way that seems to work or not to work for us depending on the situation and circumstances of the meeting. The meeting of a job applicant with the prospective employer is very different from the meeting between colleagues. The four parts are:

- assessment of the other (first impressions);
- assertion of self;
- discovery of the other;
- choice to continue.

ASSESSMENT OF THE OTHER (FIRST IMPRESSIONS)

We carry with us all our history, including our prejudices and our preferences. We use all this information to make an immediate assessment or judgement of the people we meet. We use all our senses to do this and the process is largely automatic and unconscious. It is a survival mechanism.

If our first impression is favourable we will usually want to continue the process of meeting. If our first impression is unfavourable we will tend to slow down or avoid the process of continuing to meet. Of course the other person we are meeting is doing the same thing. If both impressions are favourable the meeting continues. If either one is unfavourable the meeting will slowly come to a halt. If both are unfavourable the meeting, or coming together, usually stops. At this point, depending on the situation, the meeting could become confrontational and move into conflict.

Sometimes when people have an unfavourable first impression but continue to meet the other person, their assessment might change. However, most people place a great deal of importance on first impressions.

ASSERTION OF SELF

During the first moments of meeting we usually want to make a 'good impression' and we do this by asserting the image of ourselves that we think would make the other person see us in a favourable light: we only show the spikes we want to show. Of course if we have an unfavourable first impression of the other person then we might assert an image of ourselves that will help us to escape from the meeting.

What tends to happen is that we make a quick assessment of what we think might impress the other person and we assert those aspects of ourselves. Much of this process can take place at an unconscious level or instinctively.

DISCOVERY OF THE OTHER

If we are interested – if, that is, our first impression of the other person is favourable – we tend to move into discovering things about the other person. We do this by asking questions and sharing similar experiences, discovering what we have in common. We have a tendency at this stage to play down any differences between us. By being interested in the other person we discover more about them and they know more about us, initially at a superficial level.

CHOICE TO CONTINUE

As the process of meeting progresses we keep making decisions whether or not to continue the meeting. When both people choose to continue the process a relationship starts.

As relationships develop we assert ourselves more and discover more about the other person. Our differences appear as we show more and more spikes and with these differences can come disagreement, argument and conflict as well as respect, confidence and love.

LIVING AND WORKING IN A SPIKY WORLD

It is not always comfortable living and working in a spiky world. Comfort comes primarily from fitting in, belonging and feeling secure, and, as we know, being different and spiky can threaten this. So being spiky means that really meeting people means risking getting pricked:

- egos get pricked;
- pomposity gets pricked;
- apathy gets pricked;
- arrogance gets pricked;
- thin sensitive skins get pricked;
- vulnerability gets pricked;
- self-esteem gets pricked.

EGOS GET PRICKED

One way to look at the impact that living on the edge has is to look at how easy it is for people to have their egos pricked. Everyone has an ego, or sense of self. Sometimes people seem to meet others behind the shield of the ego and sometimes this is inflated to give others a better sense of who they are. When people meet at the edge with spikes on display egos quickly get pricked, especially inflated ones.

When people meet they usually want others to have a good impression of them, which might be quite different from a *full* impression of them. Ego is used to present the appropriate or desired impression. It does not take long for spiky people to break through to a more realistic impression. It only takes a few direct and well-aimed questions to do the trick.

POMPOSITY GETS PRICKED

When people have an inflated ego it can lead to them having an inflated sense of their own importance, but one they are not sure about. When they display this in their manner, usually by over-exaggerating the importance of deference and conformity – that is, by demanding both from others – then it is easy for them to get pricked. Of course this can only happen if the people they are meeting stand out in their full spikiness and refuse to defer or conform. Humour directed with skill at the pompous people does the trick.

APATHY GETS PRICKED

People sometimes display a marked degree of disinterest to others when they meet them. They display a sort of withdrawn self-interest and by not showing an interest in others become a focus for attention. Once again they can easily get pricked when others choose to either a) ignore them altogether or b) engage with them in a way which generates mutual interest.

ARROGANCE GETS PRICKED

When people have succeeded in having people defer to them and conform with their wishes it feeds their pomposity until they actually believe that their sense of importance is real, at which point they become arrogant. They enjoy displaying their arrogant spike and in pricking others, so it comes as quite a shock when they feel the pricks of other people's spikes.

Here again humour with a touch of disdain is very effective, but neither can be used by people who, for whatever reason, want to defer and conform. It is only when people show a different reaction that they can prick the arrogant.

97

THIN SENSITIVE SKINS GET PRICKED

Unfortunately for many people with thin and sensitive skins meeting people can be a very difficult and prickly business. It seems easier to keep their distance and to avoid as many spikes as possible. Needless to say such people do not display many of their own spikes. Sometimes the distance and silence of sensitive, often shy people is mistaken for apathy and/or aloofness. When meeting sensitive people it is wise not to progress with too many spikes or too quickly. A few gentle pricks may well get things moving.

VULNERABILITY GETS PRICKED

When people are feeling vulnerable it is very easy for them to get pricked, especially if the people they are meeting lack awareness of their vulnerability. The vulnerability such people feel may only be a temporary state and once it has passed they may well be able to tolerate a much greater degree of spiky contact. The skill when meeting vulnerable people is to check with them what seems acceptable and to operate with the appropriate degree of spikiness.

SELF-ESTEEM GETS PRICKED

Self-esteem, or good self-opinion, can be a tenuous thing for many people. Because of its tenuous nature it can be easily pricked when there is the slightest suggestion that it might be a mistaken opinion. This often happens when people are critical or belittle others, and often happens between people who seem to have a close relationship. It is as if by behaving in this way the 'stronger' person keeps the other in a more subservient or conforming role.

For people who do not have a good secure self-esteem it can be very difficult to show their 'true colours' by flexing and displaying their real spikiness.

CONCLUSION

Living and working at the edge is exciting, risky and can sometimes be painful. There is likely to be conflict and confrontation, both of which can give rise to fear. When people react with fear to difference they can, like a cornered rat, go on to the attack and respond to their own fear by trying to denigrate and destroy the source of their fear. This is what people who live on the edge have to contend with, so it is no surprise to find that many people seek the relative comfort of confluence rather than the discomfort of diversity.

12 A unique combination

INTRODUCTION

An organization is a living system but can it be shaped like clay in the potter's hand so that it stands out on the shelf? If so, then who does the shaping?

It is hard to imagine that 'an organization' can be perceived as a living thing, created by us and at the same time creating us. Yet in life this co-creating process shapes both the organization and the people who create that organization, moulding each other into shape so that the 'fit' is a good one.

Socially this moulding process is known as 'social conditioning', a process which establishes structures and boundaries for people to live together within a living system. The process occurs in every social system, every community, society and tribe that exists on this earth. As we have already discovered it is complex, and can constrain the development and visibility of uniqueness when conditioning is too restrictive and inhibiting. In organizations the process can lead to homogeneity: that is, everyone appearing to be the same. The novelty and freshness of individuality is slowly kneaded into shapes that are almost indistinguishable from each other. When uniqueness is overshadowed by conformity the spikes vanish. So what is so alluring about the conditioning process that leads both people and organizations to allow such an illuminating source of power as individuality to become hidden? The seduction stems from a fundamental need to fit in.

A PERSONALITY CO-CREATED

From the moment of conception we begin to form into unique individuals. Our spikes begin to form through both our physical characteristics and through our personalities. The very early development of a foetus is the miracle of nature at work. Right down to the minutest detail, this little person is already becoming different from any other person that has ever entered this world.

When the new-born eventually takes its first breath (or probably even before birth), it begins to interact with the world, co-creating with its family the person that it will become. The influences of both nature and nurture are at work.

The baby, born with delicate, partly formed, mouldable spikes, hooks itself on to a conditioning process – right now this is its only chance of survival, it has to 'fit in'. It must find a place of belonging, for its life depends on it. The baby is interacting with one of the most important components of social conditioning – the dynamics of the family hierarchy. This is its first of four significant relationships that help 'cast the mould':

The relationship with the family at home	fitting in for survival.
The relationship with teachers and pupils at school	becoming socially accepted.
The relationship with peers in adolescence	fitting in with peers and discovering freedom of expression.
The relationship with bosses and colleagues at work	conforming to hierarchies for professional development.

A pattern found in these four relationships can help us to understand the delicate interplay between conformity and diversity.

THE FAMILY

As mother, father, baby and siblings interact they build a dialogue together, a mutual understanding that enables them to co-exist. Baby is learning how to survive; mother, father and siblings learning how to enable survival. The parents are main-line filters through which the baby discovers its world. The different values, beliefs, behaviours, emotions and attitudes of the parents are transmitted through dialogue and behaviours. The baby learns how to fit in with the family. It finds its natural place in the sibling line, first-, second- or third-born, or wherever it belongs. Fitting in means learning social boundaries. The baby's place in the pecking order will impact on its life for ever.

The tiny baby (let's say she is a girl for now) unknowingly absorbs the powerful dynamics of the family structure. She learns from her family at a very early age that certain behaviours lead to rejection and isolation, while others lead to love and recognition. Significant messages are taken in, having a lasting, often permanent effect.

She stretches her parents to their limits at times – she is testing the boundaries. She also learns through observing, from watching others, as well as hearing and taking in instructions for herself. She learns the conforming rules of the game quickly:

- boys don't cry;
- children must be seen and not heard;
- you are not to be trusted;
- crying doesn't get you anywhere;
- get a good education and you will get on in life;
- love is conditional;
- you are a problem when you 'act up'.

The half-formed spikes are faced with a conflict between sustaining their uniqueness and conforming for survival. If her parents are over-controlling, over-nurturing or over-protective the pressure to fit in increases. If her parents guide and support the child in her uniqueness as well as clarifying boundaries to which she needs to conform, then the child will discover a very important skill: active interplay between conformity and diversity.

THE TEACHERS

The young innocent child carries her partly formed spikes into school, where casting the mould continues. Teachers play a significant role in this process and the pressure to fit in with other children increases.

As one mother recently commented 'Now that Stephanie is at school I notice that her innocence is fading. She is coming out with behaviours that she didn't learn at home.' Stephanie is discovering a new type of social conditioning as well as a new pecking order; she is experiencing the wider society without her family around. She is influenced by both teachers and her peers.

The way the teacher interacts with the developing spikes, the growing personality of the child, is critical. Each child is different and therefore needs to be respected for their difference; equally the teacher needs to create some boundaries in which to teach. If teaching is highly instructive with little space for individual expression then children's spikes will not develop well. Children begin to swallow their learning whole and regurgitate it at exams. That is not good learning. In environments where children are encouraged to develop:

- opinions rather than the 'right answer';
- principles rather than rote learning;
- science through experiment and enquiry; and
- art through exploration and freedom of expression,

then spikes have an opportunity to grow strong and sturdy.

In a system where creativity and freedom of expression are valued the child is able to continue to discover and value her uniqueness. In a system where rules and regulations are high on the list of importance, the child learns that she must conform and begins to lose sight of her uniqueness. Schools could offer a valuable opportunity to learn how to balance conformity with diversity. Teachers could increase learning by modelling good diversity practice.

In the playground

The child's new friends also begin to impact on her developing spikes. If she does not 'fit' in the playground she will be ostracized very quickly. The playground is often a tough place to bring your uniqueness into being.

Later, as she develops into adulthood and her ability to release her true self has grown stronger, she will learn that through taking responsibility for herself in society she can adapt her boundaries, enabling her integrity and uniqueness to emerge. She can take a look at the messages she swallowed when she was little and see if they still fit. If not she can change them ... or can she?

For now she conforms to the rules, occasionally challenging the boundaries through her self-expression and non-compliance. The spikes are growing, becoming more solid, more obvious; they are also slowly becoming eclipsed by the rules and regulations of the educational system.

THE PEERS

As the developing child moves into puberty she meets a different social life. Her uniqueness moves into a new phase. She wants to stand out as an individual in her own right. She wants to shine:

- She begins to experiment and test out new looks, new experiences, new images; she is innovative in her contact with the world and with her peers.
- She seeks places where her uniqueness can be set free, she wants to stand out as a person in her own right, but too much could lead to isolation.
- She dances between becoming a free spirit in her diversity and conforming to family norms and institutional rules which offer a sense of security.

As she begins to explore and test the world so her self-expression is reinforced, and sometimes ridiculed, by her peers. Managing ridicule is part of the development of her spikes. She particularly seeks social groups where her unique self is valued, and she offers the same in return. Her ability to stretch her uniqueness beyond her current limitations is determined partly by the self-confidence she established in earlier years and partly by the support she receives from her family to take new and risky steps into the world.

But how free is she? In freeing herself from the constraints of her family does she now become constrained by the behavioural norms of her social group? She has discovered how to loosen her family mould and still be herself. She now needs to find a place in society where she can belong. If she is too 'way-out' she could be rejected and find herself alone. The one thing she has going for her is the knowledge that her peers are going through this transition also.

THE BOSSES

As she moves into a working life she meets a strong influential hierarchy, and finds herself maturing into a pecking order. Key people at the top of this pecking order influence the extent to which she can develop and bring her unique self into the workplace – people whom she never sees. The opinion formers – the holders of power, status and influence – put constraints on her life that she had not anticipated. She is caught in a web where conformity supports professional development and where her 'way-outness' is less acceptable if she is to succeed on her career path.

She finds that she has to conform to legislation, to policies and procedures, to the informal norms of the organizational culture. To survive here she needs to fit in. And she is on her own now, she has to earn her own living. Money is an important factor in her life.

She is aware that this is a common pattern: only a few of her teenage friends have managed to stand out in their working lives, most of them because they decided to 'go it alone'.

She notices that she is beginning to defer to the system rather than to challenge it: she needs the job, she needs the money, and she needs to develop in her career. Instead of growing and releasing her potential into her work, she notices that people do not want to see her spikes. Her uniqueness is still with her but it is as though people do not want to see it, and she notices that this leads her to disregard the uniqueness of others. She will climb the ladder and bring some of her uniqueness into the system. The rest is lost, the visibility of her true self is clouded as the powerful force to 'fit in' increases.

CASTING THE MOULD OF THE ORGANIZATION

The uniqueness of an organization is born, and through its relationship with the world a mould is cast. The analogy with the child can offer insight to understand the co-creating process of the organization and the interplay between conformity and diversity. The following relationships, analogous with the child's development, are drawn on here to understand how the development of a unique organization changes:

● the founders (the family);

- the consultants (the teachers);
- the marketplace (the peers);
- the establishment (the bosses).

THE FOUNDERS

A new business is born, and the half-formed spikes still drying in the breeze raise the interest of the local and business community. The founders, still nervous and excited with their new venture, need to fit in *and* stand out against their competitors if they are to survive. Fitting in means learning about competitive boundaries. The half-formed spikes are faced with a conflict between sustaining their uniqueness and fitting in for survival. The pressure to conform is strong at this early phase of the life-cycle of the business, since the investment is usually huge.

The ability of the founders to bring their own uniqueness in to influence the business at this early stage is critical. The path of the organization will be deeply affected by the early phases of the business's development.

The birth of a culture

The culture of the organization is an expression of the organization. To start with there is simply the dynamics between the founders.

As people become employees of the new business the different values, beliefs, behaviours, emotions and attitudes of the founders drive and motivate the people working for them. In turn the workers bring their personalities, their history and experiences, which also influence the development of the culture. It is here that we see co-creation really taking place – the uniqueness of the culture is emerging. It is also here that people find themselves having to fit into the very culture that they co-create. The organization is already facing the tension between diversity and conformity.

As the business grows policies and procedures come into being; each new rule and regulation will chip away at the half-formed spikes, before they have fully formed. Control increases. Formal and informal norms begin to develop. The hidden messages begin to emerge. The workers learn the conforming game very quickly:

- people shouldn't show their feelings at work;
- watch your back or you might get blamed;
- you are not to be trusted if you get it wrong;
- crying doesn't get you anywhere;
- status gets you recognition;
- rewards are conditional;
- success is based on profits.

The half-formed spikes are faced with a conflict between sustaining their uniqueness and fitting in for survival.

If the founders are over-controlling, over-nurturing or overprotective of the new business, the pressure to fit in will increase. If the founders guide and support the business in its uniqueness as well as clarifying boundaries to which it needs to conform, then the workers will discover a very important skill: the art of managing the interplay between conformity and diversity.

THE CONSULTANTS

Consultants exist to help organizations learn new and different ways of operating. In many ways they are equal to the education system for children. They offer the skills and expertise for organizational learning. Some consultants offer packages which organizations purchase, others use diagnostic tools to help organizations discover what it is they need to learn about.

There are two aspects here that influence the development of the uniqueness of the organization – that is, the continued development of the spikes:

● that the consultants themselves value and embody good diversity practice;
● that the learning style is one of 'learning with' in contrast to 'telling how'.

The way the consultant interacts with the developing spikes, the growing personality of the business, is critical. Each business and its culture is different and therefore needs to be respected for its difference; equally the consultant needs to create some boundaries in which to enable learning. If teaching is highly instructive with little space for individual expression then the unique spikes of the business will not develop well. People will begin to swallow their learning whole and lose sight of it back in the workplace. That is not good learning. In cultures where people are encouraged to develop:

● opinions rather than the 'right answer';
● principles rather than rote learning;
● science through experiment and enquiry; and
● art through exploration and freedom of expression,

then the spikes of the business have an opportunity to grow strong and sturdy.

In a system where creativity and freedom of expression are valued the business is able to continue to discover and value its uniqueness. In a system where rules and regulations are flexible and not overwhelming, the business learns the real (as opposed to habitual) value of conformity. A key task of consultants is to help organizations learn how to bring these two aspects into balance.

THE MARKETPLACE

As the growing business moves into puberty it enters a different phase in its life-cycle. It needs to stand out in its own right within its industry and continue to grow. Its relationship with its competitors, suppliers and customers impacts on its ability to develop a unique and successful business:

- It begins to experiment and test out new innovations and new images.
- It expands into places where its uniqueness can be visible and valued.
- It dances between becoming a free spirit in its diversity and conforming to the norms of its competitors – too diverse and it will lose its market, too conforming and it will lose its competitive edge.

As it begins to explore and test the world its self-expression is reinforced, or sometimes ridiculed, by its competitors. Its ability to stretch its uniqueness beyond its current limitations is determined partly by the confidence of the founders, or those who hold the power, and partly by the ability of the business world to support the uniqueness of this business. If the business is too 'way-out' it will last for a while but in the long term it will not survive.

This is the biggest test that the business has yet experienced. The balance between conformity and diversity is changing inside and outside. Survival and success through this phase is impacted by the balance and interplay between diversity and conformity. Here too the leaders must learn to educate but not control.

THE ESTABLISHMENT

Here we refer to the relationship between organizations and the Establishment, the latter being the institutional authorities within our society such as the civil service, the government, the armed forces, the Church, the monarchy, the Bank of England – the formal and informal powers, the ruling classes. The mere fact that these authorities are conforming in nature implies that the relationship between an organization and the Establishment is governed by conformity. This does not mean that an organization has to lose its diversity – for example, the Virgin Group conforms to the Establishment but has managed to sustain its diversity in the marketplace. Some organizations like Marks and Spencer plc, which is governed in the main by the City and financial markets, have remained steadfastly the same for many years. Marks and Spencer has managed to remain differentiated in the marketplace despite the increased competition over the years.

When organizations defer to the system they fall into conformity. When organizations take their difference and seek to develop a relationship with aspects of the Establishment that impact on them, then they are seeking unity. Existing in the shadows of the Establishment does not mean losing diversity. What it means is that the relationship exists through active engagement, as opposed to passive conformity. Diversity that lies in the shadows can seek out light.

CONCLUSION

Both people and organizations begin their lives with their uniqueness and a need to conform to sustain their survival. Managing the balance between diversity and conformity is a delicate operation. In early years the dependency on parents, on founders, means that the spikes grow slowly. The need to survive is more important than the need to express uniqueness. As time goes by and confidence increases, a desire to discover one's unique self in the world arises. In these early phases both the child and the organization have their greatest opportunity to learn how to live with both diversity and conformity. Very few get the best from this learning, because of the limitations in education and, for organizations, the lack of skills in diversity in consultancy practice. This results in a leaning towards conformity at an early stage. As maturity is reached both the individual and the business are caught in the conformity of their Establishments. The unique combination has become eclipsed – but there is hope, it still exists in the shadows.

13 The value of novelty

INTRODUCTION

One of the greatest barriers to embracing diversity is the very belief that 'difference is oddity'. In this context 'oddity' is not acceptable. Expressions such as 'How odd!' place people and organizations out on a limb. One chief executive speaking to her marketing people said, 'I agree that we want to be different, but if we are too different we will be seen as odd.' She obviously had the view that being 'odd' was the same as being 'the odd one out'. However, oddity can also be described as novelty, and novelty is the basis of creativity and innovation.

ORGANIZATIONS NEED CREATIVITY

If your organization is like most, you are going through many changes. Your company may have recently invested in new technology. It may have plans to broaden its customer base. It may be expanding into foreign countries. It may have redesigned the business processes by which it operates. It may have flattened, delayered, teamed, re-engineered, process improved or reorganized.

It has changed and along with that change have come problems – new problems that require new solutions and new ways of thinking. It requires creativity to spawn the ideas, and risk-taking to push the ideas to innovative results.

A company can no longer survive by staying in its present state. Dr Edward De Bono, creativity educator, says:

> As competition intensifies, so does the need for creative thinking. It is no longer enough to do the same thing better. It is no longer enough to be efficient and solve problems. Far more is needed. Business needs creativity both on the strategic level and on the front line to make the shift that competitive business demands – from administration to true entrepreneurship. (De Bono 1992)

Companies must become more competitive. How? To increase the competitive advantage, companies can decrease costs, increase quality, increase speed or master innovation. The changes implemented by most companies address the first three, but not usually the last. In addition, most companies are experiencing less than half the potential of the first three if the changed workplace does not encourage creativity and reward risk-taking:

> Even when you're on the right track, you'll get run over if you just sit there. (Will Rogers)

Today managers must do more than just develop a new product or improve efficiency. They must also be creative in how they get people to work together in teams and handle the people issues in organizations. They must create a climate where creativity and risk-taking are stimulated and rewarded and mistakes are viewed as something to be learned from and not criticized. In other words an environment that fully embraces diversity.

People are creative, not organizations. An organization may be seen as a creative entity because it fosters creativity in its people. Generally a creative organization like 3M has created a climate that supports creative thinking. This climate would be OPENED, that is:

Open-minded
  Perceptive
    Equal
      Nurturing
        Encouraging
          Descriptive

OPEN-MINDED

It encourages flexibility and creativity, and invites people to be spiky. It probably allows employees to experiment with using creative approaches and techniques. Creative efforts are included in the budget. New ideas are listened to without being judged, in others words given a fair chance.

PERCEPTIVE

The company sees things from the employees' viewpoint, all 10 000 of them. There is an assurance that the work is rewarding both in a professional and a personal way. A participative atmosphere is encouraged by asking for and acting upon employees' input.

EQUAL

People are respected for the diversity each brings. Leadership techniques and

110

styles are individualized to fit the needs of each person. People's ideas are implemented well.

NURTURING

Free expression of ideas is stimulated. People are provided with knowledge through training and other learning activities that provide input for creativity.

ENCOURAGING

People are encouraged to find creativity, to search for different answers. Not only are creative efforts rewarded and reinforced, but time is built in to be creative. Freedom and opportunity for self-expression exist.

DESCRIPTIVE

Communication is very good. Clear objectives and specific feedback are basic to everything the organization does. People have frequent direct customer contact. There is a balance between structure and an opportunity for creative expression.

This 'opened' approach can be compared to the more traditional and still-to-be-found management approach which highly values control. In such environments of control the project must be done correctly, by the book, on time, and within budget, with the appropriate authority, without deviating from plan. Such environments will stifle creativity. The comments that prevent creative ideas from surfacing have been coined as 'killer phrases' by Dr Sidney J. Barnes. You have heard them: 'We've never done it that way before,' 'It's not in the budget,' 'It's not our policy.' Doing things by the book – that is, being ultra-conforming – can create an efficient organization, but certainly not an innovative one.

HOW IS CREATIVITY RECOGNIZED?

What is creativity? Mike Vance of the Disney Corporation says:

> Creativity is the making of the new and the rearranging of the old.

Creative thinking is based upon the idea that our brains have the ability to create an infinite number of ideas, combinations and relationships. Like a kaleidoscope your brain can form, re-form and re-form again multiple patterns. These patterns and combinations create the new relationships we call 'ideas'. And every human brain is different from every other human brain, although the cultures in which we live try to program them in the same way. Here are a few of the things we can do with our brains which will support creative thinking.

VISUALIZATION

Seeing the preferred future, seeing the ideal that you want to aspire to. Painting pictures of how it could be instead of only seeing how it is. Visionary thinking does not come from what we see, but from what we would like to see.

EXPLORATION

Using metaphors, analogies or symbols to question assumptions and to jolt our paradigms. As people grow and develop they learn – the brain is programmed with sets of rules, or paradigms, for how things should be. These constrain individuality and creativity. We can use our brains to ignore these old paradigms and explore new possibilities.

COMBINATIONS

Bringing various elements together in different ways. For example, the inventor of the Nike shoe sole wondered what would happen if he used a waffle iron to make a mould in a rubber sole. He combined in his brain the waffle iron and the rubber shoe sole. Then he actually did it.

MODIFICATION

Improvising, adapting, adjusting what you already have. This means not accepting any limits and just seeing what happens, which needs and gives free rein to great imagination.

The point of these strategies is to jolt you out of your day-to-day thinking and move you to think differently. There is no one 'perfect' approach. We each have our preferences. Often we go through the day on automatic pilot, allowing our habits to rule the day, hoping for the predictable and avoiding surprises. This can be good because we can become efficient and effective. The drawback, however, is that our expectation of how 'things should be' replaces how 'things could be', and this prevents us from seeing in a bigger, better, wider and wiser fashion.

WHAT GOOD WILL CREATIVE THINKING DO FOR ME, MY TEAM AND MY ORGANIZATION?

How about making your job easier? Or making yourself more valuable to the company you work for? Look around, what could be improved?

- Communication?
- Processes?
- Service?
- Products?
- Teamwork?
- Planning?
- What do customers want that they don't get?
- Faster?
- Better?
- What changes do you see coming in the future?
- Where are you going?

What about making your leisure time more pleasant? How could you mow the lawn faster, or not at all? How could you stretch your pay further? How could you make your hobby pay? How could you simplify your schedule?

Tapping into your creative energy can be fun and add a positive outlook to everything you do. You will become more imaginative in solving day-to-day problems. You can eliminate boredom, increase self-confidence and increase satisfaction in more creative personal relationships.

Probably the greatest barrier to creativity is our self-imposed limitations: 'I do not believe I am creative, therefore I'm not.'

Argue for your limitations, and sure enough they're yours! (Richard Bach)

The key to appreciating that we are all creative is to accept the premise that creativity is a continuum. It does not belong exclusively to the artists, authors and inventors of the world. Of course most of us will never write like Shakespeare or paint like Michelangelo or invent like Edison. That doesn't mean that we aren't creative.

We are all on the creativity continuum. To move further along that continuum we must first accept that we are creative and secondly acknowledge that we can increase our creative potential. Many people have told themselves for so long that they are not creative that they believe it. The very nature of the problems we may face can stop us from even attempting to find a solution. We are overwhelmed by the sheer scale of the difficulties and our creativity is stifled. The fear of failure, of not being able to cope seems to paralyse our creativity.

Breaking out of this personal belief system is difficult, but not impossible. We

113

each need to be successful at being creative. Then we need our creativity to be reinforced. We also need to take risks and to be encouraged to take risks. We need to be inspired to 'fail faster'.

HOW CAN I BE DIFFERENT AND TAP INTO MY CREATIVITY?

First of all it should be fun. A very important part of creativity involves helping people get in touch with their playfulness, wishfulness, spontaneity, stimulation, pretending, daydreaming, and free association of ideas. You could see this as getting in touch with the 'child within'.

> Children are curious. They want to make sense of things. Find out how things work. Gain competence and control over themselves and their environment, do what they can see other people doing. They are receptive, open and perceptive. They do not shut themselves off from the world around them. They observe it closely and sharply. Try to take it all in. They are experimental. They do not merely observe the world around them but taste it, touch it, heft it, break it, bend it, to find out how reality works they work on it. They are bold. They are not afraid of making mistakes. And they are patient. They can tolerate an extraordinary amount of uncertainty, confusion, ignorance and suspense. They do not have to have instant meaning in any new situation. They are willing and able to wait for meaning to come to them – even if it comes very slowly, which it usually does. (John Holt)

Secondly, it should be stimulating. This may mean considering what you can do to stimulate all the senses of sight, hearing, smell, touch and taste.

Thirdly, focus on three things: getting rid of blocks; learning new approaches to being creative, and relating the learning to your work.

Fourthly, make the learning transferable. Creativity already has a reputation of being uncontrollable, unpredictable and playful. Make sure that as well as having fun the ideas and outcomes have some practical value. The key to transferability is applicability.

And finally, your creative work should help you and your team to tap into your own individual differences which are the source of your creative ability. Enjoy yourself, get a little crazy and ... be creative!

HOW WE BLOCK OUR CREATIVITY

Within each of us exists an infinite capacity for creating ideas and nurturing them to the point of innovation. However, as individuals we have boxed ourselves in, prevented the flow of ideas, inhibited creativity and kept ourselves in the dark. You may choose to stay in the dark, or to ignite your creative spark.

Creativity does not just happen. It is not available on demand although we are all born with creative potential. The success of creativity is a learnt process. You can transform your black and white thinking into colourful innovations.

People question creativity. It is weird, strange, odd. Creative people are weirdos and because they seem very different they are threatening. People are sceptical and disbelieving about anything that seeks to increase their creativity. Yet creativity helps to conquer the challenges of change. Creativity forces people to view things in new ways. As far as we know, people are the only species capable of such diversified and complex thought processes.

> Indeed without sufficient flexibility to permit random creativity in unexpected – and non-preferred – places in the organization, many companies would not have developed new programmes, new products, or new systems. (Rosabeth Moss Kanter)

CREATIVE STYLES

We each of us have our own distinctive creative style. The effects of our upbringing, education, work and life experiences all combine to give us a unique outlook and way of responding to what happens to us. That is how we behave in any set of circumstances. Being creative is part of our uniqueness.

There are, however, certain characteristics of people we recognize as being creative. These include the following, which are based on studies of people famous for their creativity:

- They are a social bunch who thrive on visiting and talking with others.
- They don't give up and they are highly motivated.
- They worked long and hard in their field before they created something for which they are renowned.
- Their early experiences were varied and filled with the freedom to explore.
- They have an excellent sense of humour.

There are many characteristics that are linked to creativity and the following will give you a taste of some of them:

- not following rules;
- spontaneity;
- fun-loving;
- highly sensitive to own senses (sight, smell, sound, touch, taste);
- see what others don't see;
- action oriented;
- push beyond obstacles;
- not content with the obvious;
- highly differentiated;

- enthusiastic verging on the evangelical;
- highly motivated;
- high level of self-belief and high self-esteem.

One person may be creative because they are impatient, another because they are patient. One because they are bold, another because they are cautious. Whatever our personality or our personal characteristics, provided that we recognize and embrace our own diversity we can all be creative. It is sometimes just a question of opposites that might open the windows of our creativity. Whatever your creative style might be, it is yours and yours alone and it is right for you.

BUSINESS AS UNUSUAL

The ability to see things that others cannot see, to have a different way of looking at the ordinary everyday events and things that we meet all the time, is the under-lying key to being creative. When your creativity is 'switched on' all the time the results can be startling.

FASCINATION WITH THE ORDINARY

> To see a World in a grain of sand
> and a Heaven in a wild flower
> hold infinity in the palm of your hand
> and eternity in an hour. (William Blake)

Most of what happens in organizations is very ordinary, so much so that it is taken for granted, goes unquestioned and becomes ingrained in what we refer to as the 'culture'. Being creative means being fascinated with the ordinary. When ordinary events and reactions are focused on with the magnifying glass of fascination they become transformed into exciting and sometimes deeply meaningful events.

When we ignore the ordinary we ignore life. We drift along half asleep until something extraordinary wakes us up, and in this process we miss many opportunities to be highly creative.

DISCOVERING THE OBVIOUS

Have you ever noticed how when someone tells you something is obvious it does not seem to you that it is, but once it has been pointed out to you it becomes obvious?

Have you ever been given directions to find somewhere, in which you are told to look for some landmark with the fatal words 'It's obvious, you can't miss it'? And, of course, you do miss it.

116

What seems to happen is that the constant babble of thoughts that clutter our minds for most of the time obscure or deaden the information we are receiving from our senses. We are so busy 'thinking' (paying attention to thoughts) that we miss the obvious messages from our senses. Our eyes see the landmark and feed the information to the brain where it then seems to have to wait for a gap in the babble. By which time we are well past the landmark.

To discover the obvious we have to pay attention to our senses and listen to what they are telling us. We have to still our frenetic minds and make contact with our environment and other people through our senses, as well as making contact with ourselves through our feelings. We have to pay attention, and then and only then will we discover the obvious.

THE UNSEEN (BECAUSE WE DON'T LOOK)

Have you ever heard the expression 'That is blindingly obvious'? It is a strange expression but very perceptive because it is saying that something is so clear that we cannot see it. It is as if we are blinded by a veil of thought. It is not difficult to learn to look and to really take in what we see, not just the physical aspects but the other aspects of what is happening around us. A heightened level of awareness might be a good way to describe this kind of looking.

THE UNHEARD (BECAUSE WE DON'T LISTEN)

Learning to listen means stilling the constant mind babble and focusing our attention on the person who is speaking and on what is being said. By focusing on the person first and seeing them we are able to then hear them clearly. We cannot choose what we hear, unless we use ear plugs, but we can choose what we pay attention to and listening is all about paying attention.

THE UNSAID (BECAUSE WE DON'T SPEAK)

Perhaps this is one aspect of 'business as unusual' which most frequently generates surprise in people. I think this is because we all choose to censor what we say to such an extent that we often say nothing. Now censoring has its uses and as authors we are not suggesting that you should never censor. What we are suggesting is that most of us experience moments when we wish we had 'said something'.

Your aim is to bring the unspoken into the field, because it is only when this happens that you can pay attention to it. If it stays part of your mental babble it gets lost.

The expression 'tongue tied' is another of those interesting uses of language. Who ties your tongue so that you cannot speak? It also implies that you know what you want to say but cannot bring yourself to say it.

YOUR AUTHENTIC CREATIVE SELF

To be able to operate on the basis of 'business as unusual' means taking risks. All these risks are to do with revealing our truly creative selves to those we come into contact with. This is like cleaning, polishing and sharpening your spikes so that you can be experienced in all your spikiness. It is risky because we might get hurt, we might be misunderstood, we might be ridiculed and we might be rejected.

Being creative and authentic means being 'all of you'. This is much more difficult than it sounds and takes a willingness to experiment with removing some of the blocks to our natural process.

Being fascinated with the ordinary and discovering the obvious means carrying the telescope of creativity with us wherever we go. This is a magical telescope that can increase or reduce the size of things; it can help us to see things that other people do not see. The key to using the telescope of creativity is to open our eyes, our ears, our mouths and our hearts and to let the fascinating world in.

CONCLUSION

People can change. They can rediscover the fearlessness of childhood. We are what we think we are, and we can be what we want to be. Creative people will be creative, no matter which job they perform. To be creative means having the freedom to respond at every moment to your environment by doing what you want and/or need to do. Don't wait for or ask for permission. Following rules stifles creativity.

REFERENCES

Bach, Richard (1978), *Illusions*, London: Pan Books, p. 73.
De Bono, Edward (1992), *Six Thinking Hats*, New York: Little, Brown & Co.
Holt, John (1984), *How Children Learn*, London: Pan Books.

14 The desire to be the same

INTRODUCTION

We are fundamentally social creatures: we do not seek isolation and solitude like snakes or sea turtles, instead we actively seek community with others. Born into families, many of us remain in our first family for a quarter of our lives, before usually leaving one family setting to create another. Beyond our families we build up our lives in social communities. When relationships break down people often leap straight into new relationships. The idea of living in isolation and solitude, or of becoming an outcast, is unbearable. Only a very few people seek out the life of a hermit.

In conforming behaviour we can see the extent to which people will go to feel that they belong. People are willing to give up their individuality, to suppress their potential, to hide their uniqueness, and to mask their self-identity, for the sake of belonging, if that is the only way that they can find it. The need to belong is deep.

THE COMFORT OF BELONGING

At the most basic level, when we feel that we belong we feel safe, loved, cared for and nurtured. We believe that we can truly be ourselves in this place. We co-create this state in that we also contribute to the safety, love, caring, nurturing and support for others in helping them truly be themselves. We are involved in this co-creation from the day we are born.

Belonging means living harmoniously. In a diverse culture harmony comes about through difference coming together in unison with congruity. Imagine all the different instruments in the world being played together at one festival – with the musicians' skills, ear and a sense of rhythm, a melody is found. A synthesis of diversity occurs – not through instruments becoming the same, or musicians losing their different styles, but through many different instruments and many different styles playing, attuned with each other to form a whole – in harmony.

Attuned	When people are well attuned 'belonging' arises without the suppression of difference.
	[All] forces and agendas at the group, interpersonal and individual level are brought into relationship in service to the whole. They are not suppressed; they are in balance. (Harrison 1995, p. 268)
Congruous	When people are acting with congruity at a group, interpersonal and individual level, what they believe in and what they do will match. Belonging increases because people feel that they can trust each other. If you say that you care about someone and also show this in the way you behave towards them, then you are acting congruously. If you say that you care then show no signs of caring, or show signs that you do not care, then you are acting incongruously. This is also true at a collective level, with groups and organizations.
	Equally, if you act like you do not care about someone or something, and say so, then you are acting congruously. Congruity alone has no moral or ethical bounds.

So when groups and organizations are functioning well, a sense of belonging simply arises. The capacity to co-create a place of belonging is not diminished by diversity – it is different from conformity, with belongingness grounded in good, healthy contact with others.

It is the dysfunctions of people and relationships that cause a group to go off course into disharmony and discord, where a sense of belonging is lost. These dysfunctions often occur through work pressures, misunderstandings, ineffective management styles, rigid cultures, ineffective communication channels, too much focus on achieving tasks and not enough focus on people's well-being, and so on. As these dysfunctions grow so conforming cultures emerge – people will always need to find a place of belonging.

CONFLUENCE

In its extreme form, conformity becomes fixed in patterns of behaviour that are like two rivers merging; through confluence they become one river, one entity. For people this creates an illusion of belonging, and a fallacy that difficult conflict is non-existent out of harm's way. When people act in a confluent way they are agreeable and compliant, they do not rock the boat, they defer to others, and do not make a fuss or disagree. They will sometimes dress like the people they are confluent with, have their hair styled in the same way, even mimic accents. Their rewards can be twofold:

● establishing a sense of belonging for themselves;
● gaining indirect respect through identifying with significant others.

As with all fixed patterns confluent behaviour can be very subtle. For example, to consistently agree with what another person is saying puts the other person in a position where they could not argue against you! Sitting on the fence and agreeing with all parties overcomes the problem of facing conflict for the confluent person.

Yet confluence has an enjoyable and useful quality when practised in awareness: for instance, becoming confluent with the tranquillity of the countryside on a warm summer's day; enjoying togetherness with a loved one; being amongst fellow supporters at a football match; feeling a sense of oneness with the universe. These acts can be pleasurable for short spaces of time when you have made a deliberate choice. The problem arises when you are habitually confluent, manipulating your environment to avoid conflict and to fulfil your needs for belonging.

THE SPIKE-EATING VIRUS

The more that people become confluent with other people, the less they are able to gain the respect of others through their own self-identity. Their self-identity slowly becomes diminished. They become stuck in a downward spiral from which there is no escape in the current scheme of things. Conformity eats away the spikes – the healthy processes of self-identity – leading people towards unhealthy dependencies. In situations where a group of people defer to one significant person who appears to carry higher status, then everyone will become confluent with the situation. For the 'significant other' this status is powerful, which can add to the predicament – the lack of diversity, the confluence. This process is like a 'spike-eating virus' that gets into the system for *both* parties. Both parties are confluent with the predicament they are in for the same reason – both gain a sense of belonging through the behavioural dynamics that they create together. Even though the significant person is clearly different, they are colluding with confluence, even building on it, for that is how they stand out.

We all need recognition, respect and positive feedback – it is part of the mechanism that helps us discover and express our self-identity. Yet some people live in the illusion that they gain similar respect as that enjoyed by those they identify with. They are only fooling themselves. However, this game is a very clever one which many people have practised while remaining unaware of doing so for years – when the significant other becomes criticized (as gurus and key figures regularly do), the confluent person can very easily step out of the frame, or join the critics. The confluent person might not have a good self-identity but they know how to protect their weak self-esteem from being battered by critics – they dodge them through 'shifting their confluence', or by sitting on the fence.

DESTROYING THE VIRUS

The way out is very simple – to seek difference; to respect difference.

The gurus of this world who break out of the predicament are those who value the wisdom, knowledge and experience of the people they meet. They do not play on their status, indeed many do not even acknowledge such status. They are ordinary people who give as much respect as they receive, and who differentiate others as others differentiate them. They give equal status.

Fundamental change, necessary in cases where the virus has penetrated deep into the system, is more complex. Bearing in mind that the situation occurs through dynamic interactions, both parties need to change their behaviour – both the *confluent people* and the *significant figures*:

- In building their own individual and valuable self-identity the confluent person will need to learn how to take criticism and to manage conflict, as well as discovering where their differences and similarities with others exist. Self-support is critical to this process.

- Significant figures can increase their own self-identity by letting go of the status and dependency bestowed on them through confluent behaviours – they can let go of the ego-boosting comments and behaviours that they take in as their due and encourage differentiation through their respect of other people's difference (their wisdom, knowledge, abilities, skills, self-presentation, ideas, and so on). In so doing significant figures gain a more authentic sense of themselves and earn a different respect from others, a respect that is grounded in reality rather than delusion.

The term 'significant figures' refers here to anyone who is given, and accepts, status to which other people defer (give away their difference, status, power, equality). Significant figures can range from executives, managers, professionals, parents, leaders, teachers, gurus, consultants or gang leaders, to an individual in a team. Although people with role status or authority can easily fall into this trap, anyone without such status can still 'catch the virus', taking on rather than challenging deferrent behaviour towards them.

THE JOY OF BELONGING

We seek belonging in our relationships with others, in our families, communities and workplaces. Belonging is a human need. When we feel that we belong we feel cared for and valued. But what is belonging? What are our belonging needs that drive deep into the heart of our work and our lives?

Once again other people must be involved. We cannot secure belonging in solitude. So it is not just our personal desire to belong that is being played out, there is also a requirement that others want us to belong. When you are a member of any group you have a need to belong to that group, and you must want others to belong to the group as well. This probably means that there are people whom you would not want as members of your group and so inclusion–exclusion processes begin. As the picture widens so we can see how our search for belonging can so easily shift a group from healthy differentiation to unhealthy conformity. Some dynamics that illustrate the difference between healthy and unhealthy functioning groups are shown in Figure 14.1.

Healthy dynamics	Unhealthy dynamics	Some underlying issues and fears
Respecting difference	Seeking only similarities	Loss of self-identity
Encouraging difference	Discounting difference	Fear of rejection
Acting with integrity	Hiding personal views and beliefs	Fear of the truth
		Fear of isolation
Open disagreement	Disagreements get dealt with outside the group	Fear of conflict
Acting through love and caring	Acting through fear	Fear of getting hurt
		Fear of not getting your needs met
All members have something of value to offer	Wisdom exists in one or two members	Fear of making a fool of yourself
Emotions drive us	Emotions are not okay here	Fear of not knowing how to manage your emotions
		Fear of exposing your vulnerability
Managing the shadow*	Hiding the shadow	Fear of shadow emotions

*The shadow here refers to emotions that tend to be tucked away rather than brought out into the open, like anger, bitterness, anxiety, distrust, and so on.

Figure 14.1   **Belonging in groups and communities**

LIVING WITHOUT FEAR

Also identified in Figure 14.1 are some associated fears that exist in groups and teams when they are not functioning well. Many fears operate outside our awareness. It is only when we take the courage to explore around our own unproductive behaviours that we begin to see the fears that exist. Some fears are specific to individuals, others are held collectively. Fears impact on our emotions in a dramatic way – the greater the fear the more dramatic the emotion. If we accept that emotions drive our behaviour it is foolish to block these highly significant emotions, for it is as though we lose control. This in turn increases our fear and we respond in inappropriate ways to try to regain control. Typical behaviours of this nature are: being over-directive, manipulative, over-influencing, over-conforming or compliant, and so on. We all carry many fears, and to deny them is to hand over control to fate – a bit like holding the steering wheel whilst someone you do not know is operating the gears, accelerator and brakes.

So what would it be like living without fear? Your first reaction might be 'Wonderful!', but if you stay with this idea long enough you begin to realize that fear is a very important part of human existence; for a start it plays a highly significant part in social, moral and ethical behaviour. Imagine some of the people around you living fearlessly. Without fear we would live in a world of anarchy, we would lose our sense of contact with life as we know it. So living completely without fear in this way is not practical. And, as we have already mentioned, blocking our fears, pretending that they do not exist, causes dysfunctional behaviour in ourselves.

Living with our fears through awareness seems to be the answer. Learning how to differentiate between rational and irrational fear is an important first step. Noticing what drives you in any given moment and identifying the fears that lurk in the shadows of the moment is a simple but insightful exercise that you can do at any time. Knowing that you are in the driving seat managing *all* the controls can be very comforting.

FULFILLING BELONGING NEEDS

When people become over-selective and over-protective of the groups that they belong to, when the exclusion list increases and the inclusion list diminishes, and when selecting new members becomes a lengthy process, then diversity will diminish. There are three fundamental requirements for an effective group or community: 1) common purpose; 2) that group members care (see below), and 3) that difference is valued and encouraged. The wider the scope for membership beyond these basic requirements, the greater the chances for increasing, rather than decreasing, diversity. Uniting through diversity can be a very powerful and enriching process for fulfilling belonging needs.

So what about caring? What is meant here is that group members care about each other as human beings, not just for the task in hand. In our, the authors', experience caring is not a subject that is ever discussed in organizations in this manner. Yet how can people even contemplate the idea that they belong if people do not care about each other? Belonging and caring are synonymous with each other. When you feel that you belong you feel that other people care about you. When you care about others they feel that they belong. It's as simple as that!

How people show that they care – that is, genuine, heartfelt caring, rather than acting from a vague feeling that you 'should' care – brings us full circle back to the culture – does the culture support and value heartfelt behaviours? Do people know how to show that they care about others at work? Are you afraid of being misinterpreted if you show that you care? What are the norms? What would you like the norms to be?

Finding a place of belonging does not mean that you have to shed your true identity, but it does mean that you must contribute to that place of belonging, as well as finding it for yourself. That means showing that you care about your co-workers in all the wonder and excitement of the diversity that they bring to the workplace. And for those who say there is not enough time for this – to show that you care only takes a moment.

The need to belong is different for each one of us; for some it is greater than others. Diversity is about understanding such differences.

CONFORMITY VS UNITY

Conformity – provides a sense of belonging. Sometimes this belonging is real, other times it is an illusion.

– reduces conflict. Having to face anger and aggression that arises through difference is less likely to happen.

– induces a sense of being in control, therefore preventing anarchy.

– is togetherness.

– leads to predictability making relationships easier to manage.

– creates an illusion of feeling safe

and also . . .

– diminishes the boundary that once differentiated *you* from *me*.

– reduces capabilities for managing conflict for two reasons:

- boundaries are confused and so the real issues in the conflict are unclear;
- skills for dealing with conflict are underdeveloped.

Unity – increases difference. People, groups, organizations, communities, tribes and nations unite in respect of their difference.

– respects equality. There is no 'better or worse', instead there is a synthesis of diversity.

125

– values open disagreement. Conflict is managed appropriately and productively through gaining mutual understanding of different thought forms, values and perceptions.

– offers potential for co-creation, innovation, excitement, learning, discovery and experimentation.

– means living with clear boundaries

and . . .

– can lead to anarchy if appropriate diversity is not managed well.

IMAGINE . . .

Let us for a moment take conformity and unity to the extreme. Think of a team or group in your workplace of which you are a member. Working as a team or group is important to your business. Now pretend that membership of your team is conditional on all of you being the same. Imagine that each member of your team is just like you, in personality, behaviour, intelligence, style of dress, and so on. Each one is an exact mirror of you. Notice your response to this idea.

Now select a member of your team other than yourself and imagine that you and the rest of the team are expected to be like this person. You have to conform to their ways of working and being, in order to be accepted in the team, in order to belong. You have to act out their behaviour, their personality, their intelligence, to dress like them, and so on. Once again notice your response to this.

Next, imagine your team as though you are meeting them for the first time: you are all so different that you do not speak the same language, you all dress very differently, and you do not practise the same social behaviours or carry the same values. Working as a team is important to your job and to the business, so what do you all need to do in order to achieve your business goals and to fulfil your own need for belonging? Notice your response. How does this contrast with your response in the previous two exercises?

How could you apply any learning from this simple exercise to your diversity work?

It is frequently the case that when people join an organization or a group for the first time they initially conform rather than differentiate themselves. This is a healthy process when it is a deliberate and choiceful act. It will enable you to discover the norms of the group from a position of acceptance rather than from fear of rejection. However, if you continue to conform and become confluent with the group then your capacity to function well is reduced. Moving to and fro, like a pendulum, between conformity and diversity will enable you to find a place of belonging that is not hooked into confluence, and to bring your unique self into the group in a way that does not create anarchy. You discover a place of unity. This is an active process, whereas habitual conformity is a passive process.

Unity is the point at which boundaries meet. In nature this point of contact is a fertile and rich place: for instance, where land and sea meet along the shoreline a rich collection of wildlife live in co-existence. However, where boundaries of diversity make contact, potential conflict also exists – and this is disturbing. In its extreme form conflict can be destructive.

LIVING WITH CONFLICT

At times we hear people say what a beautiful place the world would be if we did not have wars constantly taking place. Of course this is an idealistic viewpoint and of course a wish for world peace is carried by many of us deep in our hearts. But we are not talking about preventing wars here, we are talking about living *with* conflict. For life without conflict – that is, conflict in the right proportions – would be a life without difference, a life without boundaries. Conflict carries energy and raises issues that are important enough for people to be in conflict about. There are times when people might not respect difference but they cannot be bothered to spare the time to sort it out; it is not important to them. Where conflict exists something important also exists for the people involved.

Conflicting viewpoints, conflicting arguments, conflicting ideas, conflicting approaches, conflicting beliefs and conflicting values are diversity in its extreme form. Learning how to live *with* conflict is very much about learning how to *live* with diversity. The deeper the conflict the more important this learning is. For example, many people enjoy a good debate over conflicting viewpoints – this is healthy conflict – but when difference runs deep, when values and deeply embedded beliefs are directly in conflict, people can very quickly find themselves in trouble – the situation becomes unhealthy and problematic. Polarization takes place, people take sides and you have the beginnings of a war. Embedded in such conflict is the fear of losing – values, beliefs, self-identity, power, material wealth, friendships, family, and so on. Many of us are not good at handling conflict in a productive way, especially deeply rooted conflict; instead we become hooked into protective and defensive behaviours. We then stop doing the very thing that can turn conflict into productive outcomes – we stop valuing difference.

KEY PRINCIPLES FOR MANAGING UNHEALTHY CONFLICT

The earlier you deal with 'simmering' conflict the easier it is to manage. Rarely does unhealthy conflict cool down of its own accord. Avoiding dealing with it and doing nothing will exasperate rather than relieve the conflict.

The following principles will help manage conflict; they are written as though you are in conflict with someone else, but they would apply in any situation:

1   To be clear what the conflict is about.
2   To articulate what it is that is important in the conflict for each of you, what you fear might happen under the current circumstances and what the conflict leaves you feeling.
3   Each of you has two viewpoints – objective (personal perspective) and subjective (personal opinion) – of the issues. These need to be articulated and heard – one at a time, without attacking or blaming each other for the situation you are in. Owning the issue for yourself as opposed to putting 'the problem' on to the other person, makes such a difference.
4   Out of this will arise misassumptions that are being made; both you and the other person will need an opportunity to correct these misassumptions.

Sometimes this is enough. Many conflicts arise out of misassumptions and misunderstandings. Once corrected the conflict resolves itself. If not, continue with principles 5, 6 and 7:

5   For both of you to articulate what you would like from the other person and what you are prepared to give, in order to begin to resolve the conflict.
6   Agree whether the issue is completely resolved or whether you need to come back to it at a later date, having had time to reflect on your discussion.
7   As you complete these principles you may like to reflect on the process as one of learning how to manage conflict – what you did well, what you could improve on, and how you might have managed the situation differently.

Sometimes it can be useful to identify how you are similar and different from each other, or what you most like and what you most dislike in each other. Occasionally people misinterpret conflict as generally being disliked by the other, when in fact the other person simply does not like a particular way that you worked in a particular setting.

The more skilled you become at managing conflict productively, the more effective you will be in your diversity skills. Avoiding dealing with unhealthy conflict situations denies you opportunities for practising these important skills.

CONCLUSION

So we discover that the desire to be the same, to live in a diversity-free world, to live a life of confluence and conformity and to live in a world without fear and without conflict is an undesirable state. In fact in evolutionary terms we would probably die out. The loss of novelty, the loss of engaging and exciting 'boundary' contact and the loss of moral values would all contribute to self-destruction. In a similar way we start destroying ourselves when we seek belonging through confluence – we lose novelty, we lose exciting boundary contact and we hide behind moral values. The way forward is to focus on developing the skills that will enable us to live with fear, to live with conflict and to nurture human desires to be different.

REFERENCE

Harrison, R. (1995), *The Collected Papers of Roger Harrison*, London: McGraw-Hill.

15 The journey starts with knowing yourself

> If there is no other, there will be no self. If there is no self, there will be none to make distinctions. (Chuang Tzu)

INTRODUCTION

Whether you are a leader seeking to improve your leadership style, a manager wanting to understand the true meaning of diversity, or an employee waiting to release your potential into the workplace, the journey starts with you. Knowing yourself is the key to effective diversity practice.

In Chapter 6 we discussed how diversity between small systems occurs through the practice of diversity within each system. Members from a small system connect and develop relationships using diversity skills. These connections are greatly increased through a good sense of self-awareness from members, who then bring this awareness into their relationships.

PREPARING FOR YOUR DIVERSITY JOURNEY

Imagine you are a traveller in a world of diversity and your journey starts with knowing yourself. What will you need on your journey?

To help you we build on a specific journey, by using the analogy of climbing. Your list of items for this particular journey could include such things as:

Skills

Climber	**You**
Learning the skills of climbing; being in relationship with the mountain	Learning the skills of people; being in relationship with others

Equipment

Climber	**You**
Maps	Awareness
Compass	Intuition
Binoculars	Observation
Ropes	Connecting with others

For Survival

Climber	**You**
Mountain huts	Reflection and sharing
First aid kit	Integrity
Chocolate	Recognizing your needs
Letting others know of your journey	Initiative

There are of course many more items that you could include. You might think of some that you would like to add for yourself.

In both journeys, yours and the climber's, the importance of knowing yourself is paramount.

KNOWING YOURSELF

There are many dimensions to knowing yourself. The two that can make a significant difference to your diversity journey are:

1 Recognizing your potential.
2 Knowing your patterns that sustain your survival.

RECOGNIZING YOUR POTENTIAL (LATENT AND UNRELEASED ABILITY OR CAPACITY)

Potential has already been discussed at length in Chapter 10. What we need to explore here is your understanding of your own potential. Knowing your potential and the range of your potential, in the context of your work, leads to easier release when circumstances permit. It also makes it possible for others to link in with your abilities and build on them.

Imagine that you are a bag of potential. In your bag are many gifts, some already opened, some still beautifully wrapped waiting for the day when they will be unwrapped and released. The gifts are divided into two distinct colours – red for abilities, blue for capacity. Each gift has a label on it informing you of the potential inside and whether it is in use or not. Make a list of all the gifts that you know are in the bag – differentiate between those already in use and those still to be opened,

	Red – abilities (depth of skills)	Blue – capacity (range of capabilities)
In use	Writing Running a business Computer literacy	Managing conflict Process consultancy Communicating with people
Not in use	Languages Composing music	Photographic Interior design

Figure 15.1   The bag of potential

which are not in use. There may be some that are still hidden, yet to be discovered: these are the invisible gifts which none of us knows we have yet (Figure 15.1).

Now add to this your secret mystery gifts. What potential would you like to be able to achieve in your life but which you never thought you had the capabilities for?

For example, it might be to learn to sing, to play a guitar, to manage a project.

KNOWING YOUR PATTERNS THAT SUSTAIN YOUR SURVIVAL

Your journey is a diversity journey, yet in truth you have been on this journey since the day you were born. You have developed your character, your personality, your style, your temperament, your uniqueness, your patterns of behaviour – all are in the frame of diversity. All the ingredients for practising diversity are there but they lie in the shadow of conformity. The patterns of behaviour that you have established for your survival and for being in the world are dominated by conforming practices. Many of these patterns are so well established that you do not even know they are there. They were established at a time when they were useful to your survival as a child. Yet rarely do we explore those parts of ourselves that were once useful but which no longer have a role to play. Instead of discarding them we store them inside 'just in case'. We play it safe. In a diverse world these stored patterns are inhibiting and diminish your efficiency, both in your work and in your life.

Like many people, you may be very skilled at noticing your spikes, or diminishing your uniqueness by creating a fuzzy boundary between yourself and others; for example:

- Putting your views on to someone else as though the other person has spoken them. Starting a sentence with 'Don't you think that …' is a classic.
- Holding back, not speaking out when you have a view, makes it difficult for people to relate to you or to differentiate themselves from you.

- Acting as though the way you do things is because you have to (someone else has created the rules and you have to abide by them), rather than because you have chosen to act in this way.
- Not attending to what other people say when it is different from what you think or feel.
- Always agreeing with what other people say, not allowing yourself to have a different viewpoint.
- Avoiding intimate or engaging contact by keeping what you really want to say hidden.

ESSENTIAL SKILLS FOR A DIVERSITY JOURNEY

Just as climbers begin their training near home rather than on the highest mountain, so you start your diversity journey close to home.

The journey that you will undertake is different. Although you may seem alone, you are never alone. Just as the mountains are the terrain on the climber's journey, people are the terrain on your diversity journey. Without the mountain there is no climb, without other people there is no diversity. As the climber is always in contact with the mountain, so you are always in contact with other people. An ability to make *good contact* is a skill that both you and the climber need to develop before you set out.

MAKING GOOD CONTACT

Good contact with the mountain is important for climbing. Good contact is attained not by wrapping yourself around the mountain but by making good points of contact with your body. You do not need many points of contact: three is sufficient, too many are a hindrance. But what does good contact mean in diversity?

Contact for the climber is obvious; it is where the body physically touches the mountain – good contact is felt by the climber. Like the climber, you too will feel a sense of good contact with other people when it is made. The difference is that the sense you feel is psychological as well as physical (e.g. eye contact). It might help to appreciate varying levels of such contact through an example. In this context 'good' means engaging, as distinct from the opposite of 'bad'. The following examples illustrate increasing contact starting with number 1, low contact through to 4, high contact.

Imagine that you are either the manager or Peter in this scenario:

1 Peter stood in front of his manager, eyes fixed to the picture on the wall behind her. He had been feeling under pressure by her all week and was fed up with it.

She was such an irritation. 'You don't seem to understand,' he said irritatedly. 'I need more time to complete this project.'

2 Peter stood in front of his manager, eyes fixed to the picture on the wall behind her. He had been feeling under pressure by her all week but knew that the customer deadline had been missed. 'You don't seem to understand,' he said, with some irritation. 'I need more time to complete this project.'

3 Peter stood in front of his manager, and caught her eye as he spoke. He had been feeling under pressure by her all week but knew that the customer deadline had been missed. 'I know that we have already gone past our deadline,' he said, realizing the position they were in, 'but I need more time to re-check the data. I want to make sure it is right.'

4 Peter stood in front of his manager, and caught her eye as he spoke. He was aware that their priorities were different: her priority was in meeting the customer's deadline, and his priority was in making sure that the data was correct before it was released. 'I realize that we have already gone past our deadline, and that meeting customer deadlines is important to you and the business,' he said, 'but what is important for me is making sure that there are no errors in the data before it goes out to the customer. I need more time to do that. Perhaps we could agree on a new deadline and I will make sure that all the checking is completed by then.'

Did you notice the difference in the level of contact between 1 and 4 from both the manager's and Peter's perspective?

Good contact for both the climber and yourself is qualitative, not quantitative. You may have friends whom you see only once or twice a year, yet when you meet them the quality of contact is so good that time is irrelevant. Frequently, too, people misinterpret good contact in relationships as being physical contact, when in fact smothering people with hugs and arranging frequent meetings can be a block to contact. You know when you have quality contact with someone; at a gut level you know because, like the climber, it feels good. You feel in control, not of the mountain or the other person, but in control of you, of the moment, of your journey, of your life. Diversity awareness enables you to have more control of yourself.

Three points that enable contact on your diversity journey are:

1 Awareness – of self (own feelings, responses and assumptions, style, character), of others (their behaviours, character, how they are different from you, your interpretation of them) and of the environment (the influences that impact on you from the environment, in other words customer needs).
2 Articulating your observations and assumptions of difference.
3 Valuing that there is a difference.

WHAT IS AWARENESS?

Awareness is an active behaviour involving *all* your senses – that includes your sixth sense, your intuition. Awareness is without judgement – judgement is a behaviour to be aware of, it is subjective. In simple terms awareness is your observation and understanding of yourself and of the social and physical environment in which you exist. Observation means using all your senses, not just visual observation.

Self-awareness is the ability to notice your own responses to the world, to know and understand your personality and your behaviour. Your awareness has a boundary. Some people have greater awareness than others. Practising diversity means stretching your boundary of awareness; expanding your range and increasing the depth of understanding of yourself, and of the world around you.

Here is an example of expanding awareness. You will notice that it carries a similar pattern to the previous 'Peter and his boss' scenario:

Thoughts	*The process of awareness*
1 You are frowning.	I notice you.
2 You are frowning. You look angry.	I notice you and I speculate.
3 You are frowning. You look angry. I think that you are angry with me	I notice you, I speculate and I make assumptions.
4 You are frowning. You look angry. I think that you are angry with me. I feel afraid.	I notice you, I speculate, I make assumptions and I notice my feelings.

Spoken

5 'You are frowning. You look angry, are you angry with me?'	I realize that my speculations and assumptions might be wrong, or different from yours, so I need to check them out.
	If my speculations and assumptions are correct I want to know what you are angry about so that I can discuss it with you, and make sure that you are not making wrong assumptions about me.

Our growth and understanding of ourselves in a diverse world is dependent on increasing awareness. Lack of awareness or blocked awareness can inhibit you in your growth as a human being and can destroy relationships. Consider the simple scenario above, and how destructive it could be if the awareness of the thinker stopped at phase 3. They would act as though their speculations and assumptions were true, and deny their feelings. It does not take many leaps of the imagination to see the range of actions that might ensue, or to see the results of this person's actions.

Awareness is like learning to walk: once you know, you cannot undo that knowing.

ON THE JOURNEY

Your journey is one that is filled with traps. These traps are not always visible to you. Vigilance is critical to spotting potential traps. How might you become trapped on a diversity journey? What do these traps look like? As the mountain to the climber hides the traps, the crevices, ravines and landslides, so it is that people carry traps on a diversity journey.

For example, conformity is a trap that arises through invisible forces much of the time; it is a phenomenon that occurs because of a dynamic happening between yourself and another person, between a group or a whole organization. Becoming more aware of yourself and your potential is half the battle. Sometimes that is enough to break the spell of conformity for you. When you change the way you behave others will change in response to you. But when you are a member of a group or large system, your influence is 'watered down' simply because of the number of people. Then, some people who resist change, who prefer the comfort and mythological security of conformity, will set traps which either prevent you from going on or seduce you into their lair, where you become entrapped again in the world of conformity. For the experienced traveller these people stand out because they hide behind a cloak. For the unwary traveller who is learning to respect diversity, they might simply appear as people with difference.

These people are travellers in disguise. There are four obvious ones that come to mind.

TRAVELLERS IN DISGUISE

The manipulator

People who manipulate skilfully negotiate control of a situation to their own advantage. In relationships this is often through the use of psychological manoeuvring. When you are trapped by the manipulator you will feel as though you have lost some control, that is, self-control. There may have been times when you walked away from an encounter and were totally bewildered as to what went on, or confused as to how you managed to get involved with something that you had no energy for or interest in; on later reflection you may have felt you had been manipulated.

On your diversity journey the manipulator might use devious means to seduce you into conforming, to giving up your uniqueness. Manipulators have many disguises that they wear:

- the hat of old friends – 'gosh you haven't changed one bit!';
- the blanket of a victim – 'they don't care about us';
- the spectacles of a sceptic – 'don't do it, they've done all this before and it didn't work then';
- the sword of a persecutor – 'look what awful things they do, they've always been the same';
- the shoes of an autocrat – 'do it my way and you won't go wrong';
- the trousers of the master – 'you always used to do it, what's different now?'.

The dominator

The dominator is a person who leads you to believe that they know best. It is a particular type of manipulation that depends on you giving up some of your personal authority to them. As soon as you do this they take the controls and drive you in the direction of *their* choosing. You no longer have control of your journey; the conditions are being laid down – the main one being that you are okay (you can have a sense of belonging) as long as the dominator is the driver. The implication is that if you don't accept this you might get rejected. Ouch!

The intimidator

Have you ever felt belittled or intimidated by someone? Some people just have the knack of making you feel small and insignificant, don't they? Well, at least compared to them. The skilled intimidator does not even have to say anything in particular, it is the way they position themselves in relation to you, the intonation in their voice, and the way they blind you with their knowledge and skills. Of course you are only intimidated when you allow yourself to be – but the intimidator always knows who is most vulnerable to their trap.

As soon as you are trapped you have diminished your uniqueness; you are probably already deferring to the intimidator – which adds to the predicament that you are in.

The conformer

Here we have the people who most resist difference. You probably already know these people well, you may even be one yourself. What is interesting is that they do not necessarily look like conforming people. Some appear quite diverse.

You may be walking along with a conformer believing that they are also on a diversity journey when after a while you feel yourself getting annoyed but you do not know why. Eventually you turn to the conformer and you notice that they are wearing clothes similar to yours, they are walking in a similar way to you, and you realize what your discomfort is about – that they continuously identify with you. To start with you are flattered, but then you become irritated:

- They do not seem to have an opinion of their own, although they always support yours.
- They always use 'we' when they mean 'I'.
- They generalize their language rather than talk in specific terms: for instance, 'It is really hot' rather than 'I am hot'.
- They are usually extremely friendly but some feel hurt when you differentiate yourself from them, they hook you back in through their emotional distress, their fear of isolation and rejection.

UNMASKING THE DISGUISE

You become trapped not so much because of the other person but because of the dynamic between you – *you* bring something that contributes to the difficulty *you* experience. Travellers in disguise can only use their hidden traps on the unwary and pliable customer; they avoid people who will see through their disguise, or who are not likely to fall into their trap.

So the first rule is to avoid traps by getting to know your weaknesses as though they are your very best friends – you must get to know yourself well.

But what do you do if you suddenly find yourself entrapped? It happens to the best of us.

The clue is in the concept of unity through diversity, valuing the other person in your differences. The two basic principles are:

1 Stand your ground, remind yourself of your uniqueness, of how you are different, and let them know this. If you wish you can also add how you value them as a person or how you value them as being different from you.
2 Reflect back to them what they are doing, how it leaves you feeling and how it interferes with diversity and effective unity. Owning your part of the predicament removes any sense of blame from the discussion.

How you do this depends on your unique style of communicating with others.

WHAT IS YOUR DISGUISE?

We have spoken so far as though the travellers are other people 'out there', but of course we all have our disguises – the people 'out there' are in fact ourselves. You may recognize all the disguises in yourself, or just one. Or you may notice different disguises, your own personal disguises that prevent others from discovering their unique selves on their journey of diversity. Knowing your disguise and the traps that you cause others to fall into is equally important information. Not knowing this can be destructive to yourself and to others in your journey for diversity.

CONCLUSION

Self-understanding is worth encouraging in your organization when you decide to take the diversity route. As in diversity there is an appropriateness to the depth of awareness that you need to promote – that is, enough awareness to increase the quality of relationships between people, and enough for people to realize the potential in themselves and in the people around them. When we seek to deepen our awareness of ourselves we inevitably at some stage come across painful insights, for instance that we too are capable of becoming a traveller in disguise, capable of manipulating others, of intimidation, of dominating and of conforming. The process of expanding awareness is therefore easier in an environment where people care about each other and support each other's learning about themselves without retribution.

16 Avoiding diversity pitfalls

INTRODUCTION

Diversity has come in for a great deal of abuse in recent times, much of it as a result of unintentional misuse of the term 'diversity' by people who have completely misunderstood what it means. Our aim in this book has been to rectify this abuse and to put diversity into its proper perspective. To do this we believe that we need to explore the pitfalls that people seem so ready to fall into in respect to diversity.

THE DIVERSITY PITFALLS

The four primary pitfalls are:

- diversity as a mistaken label for 'equal opportunities';
- diversity as a solution to 'unfair discrimination';
- diversity when it is just another form of conformity;
- diversity as a remedy for 'co-created cultures of comfort'.

DIVERSITY AS A MISTAKEN LABEL FOR 'EQUAL OPPORTUNITIES'

Diversity is *not* another name for equal opportunities. It is unfortunate that many people are confused about this and the confusion is not helped when the IPD (Institute of Personnel and Development) issue a position paper on 'A vision for the development of equal opportunities' and call it 'Managing Diversity'. The confusion increases when it is realized that 'equal opportunities' is not actually about providing equal opportunities. It is about reducing or removing all forms of unfair discrimination.

It is unfortunate and a great pity that caring people should in the first place arrive at such a damaging concept as 'equal opportunities'. We, the authors, believe in and support the efforts that have been made to try to prevent the spread of unfair discrimination, but it is a shame that this effort should have been labelled 'equal opportunities'. The very idea of 'equal' opportunities goes against the acceptance of difference and makes 'being the same' even more desirable, and hence heightens prejudice. Even John Major whilst prime minister said on prime time television that 'in this country it doesn't matter whether you are black, white, brown, or whatever'. Of course it matters. The colour of our skin is an important part of our diversity and it matters a great deal. It is this avoidance of diversity which is so often used as a basis for arguments in support of equal opportunities.

The laudable idea behind equal opportunities is that people will have access to the opportunities which they want to access without any barriers being placed in their way. The kind of barriers that equal opportunities are intended to eliminate are many and varied. Some are physical and others are psychological. The removal of barriers – that is, providing access to opportunities for everyone – is the desirable aim of equal opportunities, but the problem is that people do not want 'equal' opportunities. They want opportunities which appeal to them and which suit their unique blend of skills and character. They want to be able to make choices: they want *appropriate opportunities*.

Appropriate opportunities cannot be defined because they are different for everyone. Of course some common examples can be cited, such as wheelchair access to theatres. Because it is possible to cite some examples in this way these become the focus of 'equal opportunities'. But what about access to theatres for the unemployed at special prices? Poverty limits access to opportunities as much as disability does. And grouping people together under a single label such as 'disabled' even serves to further deny their unique individuality. The term 'ethnic' is used to describe groups other than our own, yet we all belong to an 'ethnic' (social) group.

Because we are all unique what we want or need is very different from what someone else wants or needs. Of course people share common needs, but this does not make them the same. Labelling people diminishes them, groups them and destroys the very concept of diversity, and yet labelling people is one of our favourite pastimes.

So 'equal opportunities' is actually about providing *appropriate choices* for the particular individuals involved, and preventing barriers being placed in the way of people exercising their choice with freedom. This approach supports the idea of diversity, but to put the name 'diversity' on the equal opportunities banner is to do diversity a grave injustice.

DIVERSITY AS A SOLUTION TO 'UNFAIR DISCRIMINATION'

Unfair discrimination is behaviour that results from the acting out of some deep-held prejudice that may have become embedded in a person's psyche. Legislating against unfair discrimination may curtail the behaviour and provide compensation for those discriminated against, but it will do nothing about the prejudice that gave rise to the unfair discrimination.

The basis of much prejudice is the fear of difference. As they grow up people learn from the messages they receive from parents, teachers and their peers. It is these prejudice-laden messages which create the fear of difference and which in turn breed prejudice. Diversity is not a 'cure' for unfair discrimination and neither is legislation. The cure for unfair discrimination is the removal of prejudice through education, and it is a long-term solution.

Diversity can assist in this education process by encouraging people to embrace difference and to no longer fear difference. Of course the starting point for the education process is with those people who are most able to condition the thinking of the young, namely parents, teachers and the media. In organizations the starting point of this education process is with those who condition the thinking of the people in the organization, and this is usually top management.

Diversity in itself is not a solution to 'unfair discrimination' but it can be an important part of the education process. If people experience a complete lack of fear of diversity and if they see diversity embraced all around them then they might begin to question their own prejudices and take on board the new message that being different is wonderful and not something of which to be ashamed or fearful.

DIVERSITY WHEN IT IS JUST ANOTHER FORM OF CONFORMITY

Perhaps the biggest pitfall for diversity to avoid is the pressure to be different becoming in itself a focus for conformity. 'We are all different here', although true, can become a message that people feel obliged to agree with. When this happens diversity becomes just another way of conforming. The IPD's recent campaign to increase awareness about equal opportunities, mentioned above, seeks to highlight the importance of diversity, but unfortunately they have issued a badge for people to wear to identify themselves as supporting the approach. So everyone who supports their ideas about equal opportunities is supposed to wear the same badge. Badges define belonging and conformity and it is this kind of contradictory ill-thought-through practice which diminishes diversity.

Diversity, as we have been at pains to explain, is about recognizing, honouring and embracing difference. It is not about creating some desirable phenomenon that people can support. Diversity is, therefore, not something that we want people to conform with. It is something that we want people to understand as a real existential issue for all of us.

DIVERSITY AS A REMEDY FOR 'CO-CREATED CULTURES OF COMFORT'

Many organizations do, from time to time, decide to examine and re-form their culture as if 'culture' was the colour on the office wall. Culture goes much deeper than this. Culture is the very fabric of the organization and is reflected in the behaviours of the organization's people. To change a culture means going deep into the very nature of the organization, into the values and beliefs that condition behaviour, many of which lie buried deep in the past. That such culture change initiatives often fail to have any significant effect is not surprising.

Culture is the prevailing accumulation of beliefs, values, customs, norms and behaviour patterns that define how an organization or society operates. To believe that it is possible to suddenly or quickly change such an established result of many years of 'co-created cultures of comfort' is misguided. Cultures *can* be changed, but the process is a slow one that starts with acknowledging the value and benefits that the people involved gain from the existing culture:

> The organization, a large one, wanted to examine the implications of its decision to move towards a changed culture. To help them do this a workshop was organized that invited members of the management team to work together in four groups. The first group were charged with defining what they wanted to change about the existing culture. The second group were invited to define what they wanted to keep exactly the same. The third group were asked to define what they wanted to get rid of altogether, and the fourth group were requested to state what new things they would introduce.
>
> Each group were also invited to state clearly what was different about themselves in terms of the way they worked together, their individual skills and focus, and their personal likes and dislikes. The outcome of the workshop was a realization that there was a distinct risk that the organization was in danger of dispensing with some aspects of their culture that actually were extremely valuable and did in reality help to define the organization's inherent difference from other similar organizations.

All too often organizations decide to make changes in a culture that they do not fully understand or of which they have a prejudiced perception. The people who work in an organization may not particularly enjoy every aspect of that organization's culture, but they are a part of it and by conforming with the culture they maintain and reinforce it, reaching a point where they are generally 'comfortable' with it. To make changes in such 'co-created cultures of comfort' is to risk significant resistance and damage to the fabric of the organization.

One such risky change might be the introduction of a level of diversity which the organization may not be prepared to accept. Changing the things that people do, or the way that people do things, may not be too difficult, but changing the way that people *are* is a very different matter.

144

Culture change is one way that organizations set out to make significant change that will, they believe, help to lead them to increased commercial success. The fact that this rarely happens and that most culture change initiatives fail within three years is because management teams underestimate the extent and depth of the work that has to be done. Simply establishing a list of values which seem to provide the organization with a human and socially acceptable face is far from enough.

Such a value that many organizations espouse is to 'Honour and embrace diversity in all its manifestations'. And then they continue to operate on the basis of the same old prejudices. People, especially those charged with managing organizations, need to recognize that the basic prejudices that we have all grown up with do, and will continue to, condition our behaviour whatever values and beliefs we 'say' we hold dear. Yet most organizations are unwilling to face up to and work on their in-built prejudices, preferring instead to say that they have none and that they willingly and openly embrace diversity. To use diversity in this way is tantamount to dishonesty.

HOW TO AVOID THE PITFALLS

The four diversity pitfalls discussed above are not easy to avoid. They are very carefully set and camouflaged to hide them from the keenest scrutiny. Their avoidance does, therefore, take considerable skill and a level of awareness few possess. The following approach may provide some ideas for those willing to take the risk:

1   Whenever you encounter diversity and discover that it is being used to describe equal opportunities, expose what is happening and seek to establish who is responsible and change their perception – that is, re-educate them, then work with them to introduce diversity as it should be introduced.

2   Question and re-examine any attempts to deal with unfair discrimination by using diversity and look at the prevailing prejudices which allow the unfair discrimination to exist, then set about the task of re-educating everyone involved.

3   Stop any culture change programme and carefully examine:

    – the desired outcomes;
    – the purpose of the programme;
    – the prejudices which underlie the programme;
    – what is being avoided by management;
    – what is not being said.

    Then move to improve awareness of how the current culture serves the organization and ways in which it holds the organization back.

4   Notice to what extent the organization is asking/expecting people to conform with its diversity initiatives and point out the incongruity and absurdity of this. Then introduce diversity as it should be introduced.

5   Look carefully and fully at your own prejudices and fears of difference and examine to what extent you currently support your 'co-created culture of comfort' and what it would mean for you to truly embrace your own and other people's diversity.

CONCLUSION

Avoiding the diversity pitfalls means stepping carefully and paying attention to the ways in which people talk about and respond to the idea of diversity. Here are a few of the comments we have come across:

'It's just another name for equal opportunities.'
'They talk about diversity, but they do nothing.'
'Diversity, what's that? Just another fad I suppose.'
'No doubt they will want us all to start being different now.'
'They introduce a new "corporate wardrobe" and then in the same breath talk about diversity.'

Perhaps the truth of the matter is that few people really know or understand what diversity is about or how it can impact on the life and success of the organization and everyone who works there. We hope we have helped to clarify some of this misunderstanding so that you can successfully avoid the diversity pitfalls that will no doubt appear in your way.

17 Being seen to be different

INTRODUCTION

Diversity means being seen to be different:

- Being seen to be different means *being* different.
- Being different means digging down to the foundations of cultural behaviour, to the traditions and rituals of the organization, to the collective mindset, to the paths which created standard practices.
- Being different means questioning rigid patterns of behaviour, questioning whether an identity established in the past is truly helpful today.
- Being different means a willingness to let go of old traditions in order to allow space for fresh and different practices to emerge, for a new identity to take shape.
- Being different means acting out of choice, as opposed to being entrenched in old habits or conforming to the norms of the time.
- Being different means being active participants, individually and collectively, in the co-creation of a diverse corporate identity.

In order to be seen to be different you will need to get rid of some the images that your organization carries and allow new images to emerge through the active diversity of the collective culture. You must let the world know that you mean to be different, which means both diversity inside and diversity outside: being seen to be different within the organization as well as being seen to be different by customers, competitors and suppliers. Your corporate identity will then become diverse in its expression.

Acting with integrity and consistency are the sustaining attributes of the diverse organization:

- **Acting with integrity** allows your organization to hear the voice from the heart of the organization, and behave in a manner that is true to its values. This means following the steady flow of change.

- **Acting with consistency** means doing what you say you will do without contradiction; for instance, behaving in a manner that supports the espoused values and the purpose of the organization.

Being consistent in your behaviour means recognizing the motivations and mindsets from the past that carried a purpose then, but which today offer little value to the business. So embedded are these motivations and mindsets at times that they unwittingly bring resistance to change. This is when inconsistencies begin to emerge – when new thinking and new practices are introduced without raising awareness of, and letting go of, old practices, ingrained behaviours and habitual ways of working.

FROM UNIQUENESS TO CONFORMITY

THE RISE AND FALL OF M & M LIMITED

M & M Limited grew up from a little back-street shoe shop into a large national retail business. The chairman of M & M Limited, Ms Mindset, is the niece of Mr Motivation, the cobbler who once set up the business in that little back-street shop. Mr Motivation was successful because of the high quality he offered his customers; he was rigorous in the way he ran his business and in the way he cobbled his shoes. Because of this, within two years of setting up his business he stood out as the best cobbler in the county. It wasn't long before he was renowned country-wide, with shops in every major town and city. He ran his business with pride, and to stand out even more he had distinctive uniforms made for his shop managers and shop assistants.

As the business was growing he noticed that people were copying him. Other shoe shops were popping up with different uniforms for their staff. And he had to admit that the shoes that other cobblers were producing were also of a high standard. Mr Motivation was one of the first to become a shoe manufacturer, still retaining the quality that was his pride. But slowly he was losing his uniqueness, and the business started to go downhill. With some sadness and despondency he handed the business over to his niece, whom he knew had always respected the way he had run the business. Mr Motivation quietly retired.

So Ms Mindset took over a declining business; the competition was increasing rapidly. There clearly was a change in the marketplace. Ms Mindset had watched her uncle with interest over the years and had recognized the pride employees had expressed when given their uniforms – so she decided to change the uniforms for something new and fresh. She reminded the staff of the traditional ways of working that had got the business where it was and the importance of sustaining this. She encouraged managers to become more rigorous with management and administration because a successful business had grown out of such rigour. She brought in consultants to help. She had heard of many new initiatives for developing organizations and decided to try out a few; after all, that is what the competitors were doing.

The business picked up for a while but then started dropping again, faster than ever before. M & M Limited was unable to sustain its individuality, its pride of place, and eventually went out of business.

The detail of M & M Limited is brief but carries familiar patterns for many businesses today. Diverse in its origin, the firm got caught up in the economics and competition of an emerging industrial climate and was unable to sustain its unique position.

Let's relate this scenario to the list of points at the beginning of this chapter:

1   Being seen to be different means *being* **different**   M & M started off from a unique position: it was different in the quality of its products and the rigour with which the business was run. Mr Motivation was *being* different in the way he worked as a sole trader. These differences carried the sustaining values of the business – quality products and high-standard business practices. But diversity has a fluidity that must be engaged. Neither Mr Motivation nor Ms Mindset allowed the diversity of the business to flow and change over time; they both kept going back to the old practices believing that these practices would sustain the business for ever.

2   Being different means digging down to the foundations of cultural behaviour, to the traditions and rituals of the organization, to the collective mindset, to the paths which created standard practices   What Mr Motivation and Ms Mindset had not realized was that the uniqueness of a successful business one year becomes a norm the next for other businesses, in a highly competitive business world. Being different does not mean letting go of deeply embedded values if these are still important. Values are the foundation of a business and inform employees *how* to carry out their work both strategically and in practice – it is not values that rigidify working practices. Yet these values created a path of traditions, mindsets and beliefs about how things *should* be done.

3   Being different means questioning rigid patterns of behaviour, questioning whether an identity established in the past is truly helpful today   For whatever reason Mr Motivation and Ms Mindset did not question their image, or their practices in the changing climate.

4   Being different means a willingness to let go of old traditions in order to allow space for fresh and different practices to emerge, for a new identity to take shape   When Ms Mindset took over the business she did not let go of the old traditions established by her uncle, an approach which would have allowed her own individuality to influence the direction of the business.

5   Being different means acting out of choice, as opposed to being entrenched in old habits or conforming to the norms of the time   Ms Mindset did not stop and consider the possibility that she had choice in the way that she ran the business. As the saying goes, 'old habits die hard' – well, they do when people hold on to them.

The second mistake that Ms Mindset made was to believe that what her competitors were doing she also needed to do in order to survive. She conformed to the norms of the time, and called in consultants who brought along their services and products; products that appeared to offer something new for the business. She went through the list, did them all, but still could not achieve what she wanted to achieve.

6   Being different means being active participants, individually and collectively, in the co-creation of a diverse corporate identity   Ms Mindset failed to find the support that would help her tap into the dormant wealth of diversity, knowledge and experience that already existed in the business. She acted as a passive receptor to the services and products that consultants brought to the business, rather than actively engaging with employees in the belief that they could offer some value in the direction of the business.

FROM UNIQUENESS TO UNIQUENESS

Let's rewrite the M & M Limited story in a way that would have fully supported diversity in the evolutionary path of the organization.

THE SUCCESS OF M & M PLC

M & M Limited grew up from a little back-street shoe shop into a large national retail business. The CEO of M & M plc, Ms Mindful, is the niece of Mr Motivation, the cobbler who once set up the business in that little back-street shop.

Mr Motivation was successful because of the high quality he offered his customers; he was rigorous in the way he ran his business and in the way he cobbled his shoes. Because of this, within two years of setting up his business he stood out as the best cobbler in the county. It wasn't long before he was renowned country-wide, with shops in every major town and city. He ran his business with pride, and to stand out even more he had distinctive uniforms made for his shop managers and shop assistants.

As the business grew he noticed that people were copying him. Other shoe shops were popping up with different uniforms for their staff. And he had to admit that the shoes that other cobblers were producing were also of a high standard. Mr Motivation was one of the first to become a shoe manufacturer, still retaining the quality that was his pride. But he recognized that competition was increasing and that if the business was to survive he would have to look for different ways of standing out in the marketplace. He wanted to retain his values, but how could he do this and be seen to be different? How could his business look different from other shoe manufacturers, feel different for both customers and staff, sound different and even smell different? He realized that the business was 'his' business, that employees worked for him rather than for themselves, and that he needed to let go of some of the old traditional ways of working.

The first thing that he did was to bring his young niece, Ms Mindful, on board to help him in his venture. She was alert to new ideas, sharp in her awareness and very distinctive in her personal style. He felt that she would bring colour and vitality to the business. He also felt that she could engage with the workers in a way that could involve them in the business. He had never been very good at that.

The first thing that Ms Mindful did was to bring together 24 people, a cross-section of management and staff from all aspects of the business – retail, marketing, manufacturing, finance and administration, purchases, property management and customer service. Her objective was to find out what the employees thought about the company and what it needed in order to be different. Through these 24 people she invited all employees to contribute. What she discovered was that, contrary to her uncle's beliefs, employees wanted to contribute more to the running of the business; above all they wanted to discard the uniforms and establish an image that carried the values of the business *and* the imagination of management and staff. Ms Mindful realized that management particularly needed help to make this transition, so she called in experts from outside who could offer support and the re-education needed to achieve the collective objective of the company. She was choiceful in selecting this support; it was important to her that the co-creation of a new business out of the old would not be through dependency on the outside, although interdependency would be acceptable.

As time went on, the atmosphere in the organization changed; people began working and connecting in a different way, their attitudes towards each other and the business were more positive and optimistic. Some people left because they didn't like working in this way, others carried on as they always had done, and that was okay too.

As the new business began to take shape Mr Motivation took more of a back seat, although with some reluctance, to retire completely – he was enjoying the renewed energy that his niece was evoking. In particular he noticed that each division of the business began to emerge with its own identity, and the sections within divisions seemed to have some autonomy of their own. He visited all the shops over a period of time: each one carried both a symbol of the business and their own unique identity, an identity that was in character with the town or city in which they existed. Sometimes the difference was simple, like having informal displays of fresh flowers from a local florist in the shop. Others were more sophisticated in their ideas: one shop had a dancer every Saturday outside the shop, entertaining customers and wearing shoes from the shop. The shoes took on new and different styles, administration repositioned itself in the company with open offices, and the manufacturing process changed significantly. Products were no faster in the production process, but people seemed much happier and more alert to emerging problems as they arose. The quality of products and business practices was sustained, and M & M carried a buzz that had not existed in the past.

Mr Motivation particularly noticed that M & M had developed a different relationship with its suppliers: small mixed worker groups held regular meetings with suppliers every month to discuss supply-related issues and their business relationships. Out of this had emerged new ideas for working more efficiently together. The meetings had been mutually beneficial.

Mr Motivation was curious: why hadn't he thought of engaging management and workers in this way, or come up with the innovative ideas that workers were presenting? And how did the company manage to support this level of diversity without breaking into anarchy? He knew that mistakes had been made since his niece had taken over, but there had been no real disasters, and all the mistakes had led to useful insights in working practices. His questions were answered when he found a book called *Profiting from Diversity* on his niece's desk.

Today M & M plc stands out in a unique and novel way both internally and externally. The two things that remain are the deeply embedded values of quality products and quality business practices. Well, there is a third: the sign that once marked the very first shoe shop in the little back street now stands in pride of place at the entrance of the Main Office, as a reminder of the importance of being seen to be different.

A DIFFERENT CORPORATE IDENTITY

Being different is what leads to a different corporate identity. To achieve this M & M plc worked with diversity in two ways:

1 Through the informal network of employees, the informal systems of the business; for instance, *being* different with employees, encouraging them to share their views on how they thought the business could be improved and to keep this system flowing.

    Here are some more ideas to make shifts at this informal level:

    - shifting from being helped, to helping ourselves;
    - shifting from teaching how, to learning with;
    - shifting from power of control, to servant leadership;
    - shifting from power over, to power with;
    - shifting from dependency, to interdependence;
    - shifting from team leaders and followers, to team players;
    - shifting from performing, to learning;
    - shifting from doing it differently, to being different;
    - shifting from doing it quickly, to doing it fully;
    - shifting from planning, to experimenting,

    and so on.

2 Through formal business relationships; for instance, *being* different with suppliers and seeking a co-created relationship with consultants to support change.

    Other formal relationships could have been:

    - moving from being competitive, to being collaborative with competitors;
    - moving from being a business, to being an excellent business for customers;
    - moving from being a system, to being a community with employees;
    - moving from being a client, to being in partnership with accountants and banks;
    - moving from being a 'sore thumb', to being an integrated part of the local community,

    and so on.

But this is not all, for these new practices can be revolutionary for an organization, and can become established working practices that offer distinction. Yet these practices, these ways of working, both formally and informally, can once again become fixed and rigid, losing the uniqueness that they once provided. The secret is knowing that diversity and uniqueness are in constant change with the environment. Remember in Principle 3 in Chapter 10 we talked about different potential emerging under different conditions. It is these changing conditions that lead to different aspects of the corporate uniqueness becoming visible as the environment around them changes, as the market changes, as the world economy changes. Diversity and uniqueness are never static.

CONCLUSION

Being seen to be different is more than what it seems. When seeking new identity people often engage in *doing* things differently instead of *being* different. In truth we need both, yet in many organizations 'being' is not valued or rewarded, whereas 'doing' is. Consequently the organization becomes entrapped in activities, in doing more of the same, or in doing what others are doing, as in the first M & M Limited scenario. The worse the situation gets, the greater the fear of failing and the more people engage in repetitive activities, albeit that they try to do them differently. Stepping out of this paradigm into valuing both doing and being is a step towards change and a step towards a new and unique corporate identity emerging. To prescribe a new identity is to suffer from old paradigm fixation; to allow a new identity to emerge out of being different is both sustainable and profitable.

18 Corporate diversity

INTRODUCTION

Our message about diversity is intended both to provide you with an insight into what diversity really means and to offer you ways in which you can embrace and implement diversity in all its fullness. Many people recognize diversity at an individual and a small-system level but struggle to see how it can be applied at the corporate level. This is understandable as the tendency has been for organizations to encourage the development of 'co-created cultures of comfort' and to play down diversity.

Corporate diversity is not only possible, it is, we believe, essential for corporate survival as we enter the third millennium. Here are a few of the ways in which organizations can choose to adopt corporate diversity.

TAKING A DIFFERENT VIEW IS QUITE DIFFERENT FROM TAKING A VIEW OF DIFFERENCE

When organizations take a different view of their products and services and their activities they can produce innovations which surprise their competitors. Here are a few examples for you to think about.

The supermarket (Waitrose) that decided shopping was a hassle and provided a quiet, calm and easy environment to shop in – not competing solely as others do on price but on providing hassle-free shopping. Their stores include an area to sit, have snacks and read the newspapers provided, toilets and facilities for children, and parking areas for mothers with children. This is an approach that means extra tills are opened as soon as queues form, staff appear 'from nowhere' to help people who seem to need help with packing, and there is a variety of trolleys with 'quiet' wheels that go where you want them to. They have a store card that is also a credit card.

The petrol company (Texaco) that decided to experiment with forecourt shopping because they realized that people who stopped to buy petrol would buy other things if they were offered the opportunity to do so. Most petrol stations have now copied this innovative idea and some have extended their shops to provide an important facility for the local community as well as passing motorists.

The telecommunications company (Orange) that decided to give away 'free' mobile phones when people signed up with its service. The company clearly took the view that it was their service that was going to make money and that for people to use the service they had to have a mobile phone. Simple thinking, really.

And what about the bank (First Direct) that decided it didn't need branches to do business? This has been a very successful innovation, which others are following, because someone looked at the market for banking services in a different way.

COUNTERACTING THE ECONOMIES OF GREED

Greed grows when it is fed. Greedy organizations operate at legal and moral boundaries. Barings was a good example of a greedy company that fed greedy staff who were then given licence to push the boundaries of what was acceptable, and of course they paid the price.

Greed robs organizations of resources and people of dignity. Paying greedy investors large dividends and greedy managers large salaries and bonuses takes resources from the organization and takes the dignity from the managers whose greed is rewarded. The whole pressure becomes short term, quick fix, quick profits and then quick exits for both managers and speculators.

Fat cats die young. There are very few happy, healthy 'fat cats'. Rich living is physically and morally unhealthy. Broken marriages, drugs, alcohol, heart attacks, strokes and suicide are some of the rewards of greed that remain largely unspoken of.

Paying for value is a concept that many organizations, especially greedy ones, do not understand. Share options rarely, if ever, reward value for the organization. Share price increases only remotely and indirectly benefit customers and employees. The reason for share price increases may also have nothing whatsoever to do with the activities of the managers and directors of the organization. In a bull market share prices rise, in a bear market share prices fall, regardless of the success or otherwise of the organization. Rumours and speculation also affect share price. Paying for value requires attention to a simple question: 'Have the personal efforts of the individual or team added in a measurable way to the long-term value that the organization provides for all its stakeholders?'

Putting in instead of taking out is the first principle of investment. Investment merits a fair reward in relation to the size of the investment, the length of time the investment is made and the degree of risk involved. The basic idea of investment is the belief that such a fair return will be received over a period of time, and that this might even be exceeded and a better than expected return achieved. Greed at all levels prevents this form of investment from being made because it does not produce a big enough return fast enough to satisfy the market, so the money is hard to find. Special long-term investment instruments are needed that have no early return but an excellent long-term result.

BUILDING FOR THE FUTURE

Building for the future is not popular at the present time. Appropriate long-term forms of investment do not exist to make building for the future worth while. Directors approaching retirement are not interested in long-term developments that will not pay off in their working lifetimes, especially if they have short-term share option schemes.

Building for the future does not slow down reactions but stagnation does. The fact that markets are fast changing and that organizations have to react quickly makes it vital for long-term investment in people and infrastructures to be made, and such people retained and rewarded appropriately. Organizations that do not invest and change stagnate.

Building for the future defeats greed because gluttons cannot wait to be fed. However, what can happen with such an approach is that careful management can lead to organizations becoming ripe for take-over and being plundered by corporate raiders. So the answer is to make it very difficult for this to happen by creating special share schemes and conditions that make it legally very hard for this to happen. Pirates will steer clear of ships that are well armed and ready to repel boarders.

Building for the future focuses attention on the impact of what we do today on what happens tomorrow. The view is always on what happens next and what can be done now to achieve what we want in the future. Information about the past is only of passing interest. What can be learned from what has happened has already been learned before the figures arrive.

Building for the future ensures sustainability. The only way forward is one of sustainability. Whatever is used now has to be used in a way that sustains the supply for the future. When trees are felled other trees have to be planted. When things are finished with they need to be recycled. Resource consumption has to be minimized, especially packaging. Organizations should try to use resources that can be replenished in favour of those that cannot.

TREATING PEOPLE AS PEOPLE AND NOT AS HUMAN RESOURCES

The term 'human resources' should be eliminated from use right now. The authors have no idea who first came up with the term, but it was quickly latched on to as a way of avoiding dealing with real people. Human resource managers do just that, they manage human resources. They carry out 'head counts', workforce planning, age profiles and turnover figures, and forget that they are talking about individual human beings.

People should be seen and treated as people. It is hard to work with people without seeing them as individuals and yet many managers seem to be able to do it. People should not be seen simply as sets of competencies but as real flesh and blood people with moods, family problems, physical ailments, one minute excited and the next quiet and reflective. People are people no matter how we try to limit them and stop them bringing feelings and emotions into the workplace. They respond better and perform better when they are treated as people. We all do.

Bring a loving TOUCH into the workplace. It is perfectly possible to operate in the workplace in a way that is warm and caring for others. It is not easy because it is not standard practice and it is often not welcomed by the 'system'. However, when we operate with a loving TOUCH it makes a huge difference. In this context TOUCH stands for Trust, Openness, Understanding, Consideration and Honesty.

People achieve more and perform better when they are treated as people. The evidence for this is all around us in the workplace, and research shows that organizations which treat people with a loving TOUCH have less absenteeism, higher quality, less rejects, higher levels of customer satisfaction, low staff turnover, higher morale, and as a result higher profits, plus a better public image.

WORKING IN THE PRESENT TO INFLUENCE THE FUTURE

Now is the moment when everything happens. Post-mortems provide data about what has already happened and this might be helpful in our learning, but when it is done to level blame it is counter-productive. Many organizations operate a blame culture where the safest course of action is to avoid any risk and maintain the *status quo* – keeping your head down, or not rocking the boat. When people work in the present and take responsibility for what they are doing then there is hope for the future.

Today's decision is tomorrow's success or problem. When people make decisions they can only influence the future. This might be the immediate future or some later event. What can never happen is that a decision taken today influences the past. Obvious you might say, but how many people take decisions today based on trying to avoid something unpleasant that happened in the past? Learning from mistakes is one thing. But making decisions based on historical conditions which will probably never be repeated is not helpful.

Today's solutions are tomorrow's problems. When people rush to resolve problems they often produce answers which become tomorrow's problems. Going round in circles in this way happens because people do not stop to look carefully at the problems they face and become fully aware of the implications of any action they might take. This is another version of the quick fixes mentioned above.

REMOVE TRADE DEBTORS AND CREDITORS FROM THE BALANCE SHEET

Funds transfer means we can pay straight away: COD (cash on delivery) and CBD (cash before delivery) are perfectly feasible without using cash in its traditional form. You might think that this is taking being different to extremes, but is it? Trade debtors and creditors are an historical hangover from the days when it was unsafe to carry and handle cash. This is no longer appropriate and trading companies no longer need to act as bankers. Of course organizations might choose to continue to act in this capacity, but think of the lower prices that those which opted not to could offer customers from the administrative savings they could make.

There would be no sales and purchase ledgers and no costly procedures for chasing payment. Nor would there be any commercial bad debts. The banks would have to carry the risk and the cost of funding organizations which did not have a good cashflow. Those organizations which presently use factors to collect their money for them know the advantage of not having trade debtors and they are prepared to pay for it. If customers paid at once then they could have the savings directly.

UPSIZE BY EMPLOYING MORE PEOPLE WORKING SHORTER HOURS

Downsizing has gone too far, and it does not work anyway. The announcement by the chairman of British Gas that they had taken downsizing too far and that customer service was suffering says it all. Organizations need people in order to do what the organization is there to do. What has happened is that somewhere along the line payroll costs have been seen as the place where savings could be made quickly and effectively by sacking people. The belief is that the remaining people would be happy to take on the extra work for more pay. This once again works on the greed principle. However, people can be and are only willing to go so far. When they reach their limit they either leave, fall sick or cease to perform effectively. Fewer people working harder for more money damages the individual and society. Society is damaged because when people are sacked the social costs of unemployment have to be carried by society whilst the savings go into the pockets of the shareholders and speculators. In addition high unemployment leads to more social problems and more crime.

Upsizing provides work for people and is good for individuals, the organization and society. In addition, much to the surprise of those organizations which have upsized, productivity increases. The reasons for this are simple. People who work shorter hours are more effective and less tired during those hours. Having more people working shorter, more flexible hours makes better use of physical assets. With more people there is the opportunity for more diversity and hence creativity and innovation. Organizations can be encouraged to upsize by the state providing employment allowances. Organizations can also be discouraged from downsizing by having to carry the social costs of doing so.

INVEST IN REPLENISHING THE ENVIRONMENT AND NOT IN PLUNDERING IT

Organizations that use raw materials, whether directly (quarrying/lumber/oil) or indirectly, should consciously replenish the environment. If they cannot find a way of doing this directly then they should be charged a hefty extraction tax at the point where they distribute their profits.

Organizations should invest in measures to eliminate pollution or be penalized by a charge on distributable profits and capital gains so that society can clean up the mess they make without having to carry the cost for so doing.

Minimizing resource consumption – for example, through such methods as minimal packaging, paper reduction, recycling or replacement thinking – could be given more attention. Not only would this save money for organizations that do this, it would also improve their public image through their demonstration of their social responsibility.

REWARD PATIENT INVESTORS AND DEFEAT THE SPECULATORS

There are two types of investors – patient and impatient. Patient investors look for either long-term capital growth or income or both. They are prepared to wait for their returns and to take them in a sustainable way – that is, as the organization can afford to pay them. Sometimes patient investors do reap excellent rewards from having chosen to invest in very successful organizations such as Microsoft and Intel.

Impatient investors look for high, fast returns from plundering assets, which might and often does include the skills of the people actually creating the profits. They do this by encouraging directors to seek very high, short-term profits from downsizing, reduced capital investment, and so on. Impatient investors only hang around long enough to make a killing and then off they go with no interest in the organization, its products, its customers or its people.

Speculators are *not* investors – they gamble on the rise and fall of markets and have no motive other than to turn a profit on their 'deals'. Of course if the organization is so constructed that their shares cannot be easily traded they can defeat the speculators. This may limit their access to funds, but any successful organization can usually find the funds it needs. Whilst the markets encourage speculators there will always be greedy people ready to pick off the first tasty morsel they come across.

STOP TALKING ABOUT PEOPLE AS ASSETS AND START TREATING THEM AS ASSETS

Many organizations talk about 'investing in their people'. One of the most oft-quoted examples of this is 'Our people are our greatest asset'. The organization then goes on to treat them as anything but. Human asset accounting has been around for quite some time and yet the value of people does not appear on the balance sheet of many organizations. Football clubs are an exception to this because their players are clearly of marketable value and the amounts are so huge that they have to be accounted for. Few other organizations have the same issue and yet the value of their people is often considerable.

Treating people as human assets is both practical and effective. Instead of employing people and paying them a month in arrears, as is the norm, organizations could invest in them. They could do this by paying them a signing-on fee of, say, 50 per cent of their annual salary for each year of their contract. So individuals on a three-year contract at an annual salary of £30 000 would receive a signing-on fee of £45 000. They would then receive the remainder of their salary on a monthly basis. The signing-on fees would have to appear in the balance sheet as a capital investment and be depreciated as people worked out their contracts.

At the end of the three years, if a new contract is offered there would be another signing-on fee. This approach would greatly help people to change jobs, maintain some organizational allegiance, and make the organization more aware of maintaining the value of its people.

Contracts and transfer values could become as common in normal work as they are now in football. If people want to move part-way through their contract then the new employer would have to pay a transfer fee or individuals would have to pay it themselves out of their new signing-on fee. Wages and salaries are an archaic

161

form of rewarding people that no longer fits the needs of the modern world. It is time that the whole question of reward for personal effort and imagination was shaken up and rethought.

WHO AND WHAT ARE STAKEHOLDERS?

Take a different view of stakeholders and something changes:

- Customers as fans.
- Suppliers as supporters.
- Employees as investors.
- Managers as coaches.
- Directors as servants.
- Bankers as suppliers.
- Shareholders as bankers.

CUSTOMERS AS FANS

When customers become fans of the organization the relationship changes from one of simply buying the organization's products and services to one of supporting the organization. This is more than customer loyalty. Being a fan means believing in the organization and what it stands for and how it behaves in respect to the local community and the environment. Fans believe that the organization shares the same values as they do and so a mutually supportive relationship develops.

SUPPLIERS AS SUPPORTERS

When suppliers become supporters they see that their own activities flourish because their customer flourishes. They are prepared to go out of their way to help and mutually supportive relationships grow and develop. Just-in-time systems are one indicator of how suppliers can support and trust their customers.

EMPLOYEES AS INVESTORS

Most employees invest more in their organizations than the majority of the shareholders. Employees invest their time, their skills, their futures and their livelihoods in the organizations they work for. Shareholders invest their money, but few of them invest everything they have, as most employees do. It is time that organizations placed a true and real value on their people and then treated them accordingly.

MANAGERS AS COACHES

Managers are in the privileged position of being given the responsibility for supporting and guiding a group of people in the achievement of their objectives and the realization of their personal worth. This is an important role and requires managers to be able to coach their people effectively. It is only when the people for whom they are responsible perform that managers perform. So coaching and helping people to perform is the manager's primary and most important role.

DIRECTORS AS SERVANTS

Directors are or should be the servants of their organizations and especially of the people who work there. The principal role of directors is the governance of the organization in the interests of its stakeholders. This can only be achieved by providing the people in the organization with the environment and resources they need to perform. Directors are then the servants of the people they employ.

BANKERS AS SUPPLIERS

Money is a resource and banks are the suppliers of the resource. They are paid for what they supply. Unfortunately they usually want it back at some stage. This is a shame because organizations have usually used the money to invest in their activities and it is not easily available, especially at short notice. If banks made money available on a permanent basis – if, for example, they were money suppliers and were paid regularly the cost of the money (interest) – then the whole financial system would be much more stable and organizations could invest for the long-term future growth of the business. In such a situation organizations could rely less on share capital and not be subjected to the speculation and take-over vagaries of the current financial system.

SHAREHOLDERS AS BANKERS

If shareholders took as much interest in the affairs of the organizations in which they invest as bankers do, they might be able to both help the organization and protect their investment. Instead they often leave the whole control and management to directors who put their own personal short-term interests before those of the organization's stakeholders. The annual general meetings become nothing more than the self-perpetuation of dynasties of directors who pay lip service to the concerns of their shareholders.

CONCLUSION – A DIFFERENT VIEW OF THE ORGANIZATION AS ONE OF SERVICE

Diversity in itself is not enough because it is just a statement of reality. Diversity exists because every human being and every organization is different. What matters is that we see diversity as a means of enhancing the lives of everyone. This will happen when organizations see themselves as providing a service that allows people to explore their uniqueness as fully as possible. It is organizations that serve us and not vice versa. Organizations are human inventions for helping us to reach for our potential and fulfilment. If we let the inhuman organizations and systems that we have created take over then who knows what will happen. Diversity as a recognition of our individuality and uniqueness is vital. It will help us to put organizations in their place, as being of service to us.

19 Delivering diversity

INTRODUCTION

We hope that by now we have convinced you that there is a strong link between diversity (recognition of individual uniqueness) and performance. If people are able to be fully themselves and to access and use all of their existing skills and potential, then they can perform at their very best.

Of course saying this is far easier than achieving it. But no matter how hard it may be to deliver diversity, anything and everything we do which moves us in the direction of diversity is a step forward and well worth the effort.

PERFORMANCE AND DIVERSITY

In Chapter 11 we talked about people as spiky shapes that depict their uniqueness. The outer limits of their individualities is where all the creativity and excitement is, and it is where people perform at their best. When people compress their 'spikiness' into some more acceptable form they limit themselves. When organizations demand such conformity they limit their people, and what becomes acceptable is only a fraction of what is available.

The spiky diagram shown in Figure 3.2 can be pictured as representing an explosion of personal energy, with the spikes being the outer reaches of the energy, which is where the authors believe real contact is made with people and the environment and where people 'perform to their limits'. If the energy is contained by social and organizational norms (culture) the energy is not available for people to access and use when they perform.

Because we are all different we will present different shapes to the world. Our energy will flow differently and our experiences, interests and desires will be different. One way to deal with this is to try to limit and reduce difference by getting people to conform to some corporate view of how things should be – a view which is often based on prejudice, particularly the prejudice of past and present corporate leaders. In this way individuality is played down and the organization demands allegiance to the flag. Their corporate identity is what they stand for. It represents who they think they are. Everyone who works for the organization is expected to uphold these corporate values. They are expected to appear as members of the organization and whilst doing so to put the organization before themselves.

This presents people with a dilemma. Do they accept these corporate values because they believe them or because they want to keep their job? If they seek to express their individuality by being different they will stand out and probably have to get out. There is a basic human desire to belong which can tug people towards conforming; they might choose not to stand out if the latter possibly means being rejected and isolated. This is the safe approach and it limits us in all kinds of ways.

INTEGRATING CONFORMITY AND DIVERSITY

The authors are not attempting to suggest that we have to have either conformity *or* diversity, but rather that it should be conformity *and* diversity in some appropriate balance. People need to be able to find the comfort of belonging and being accepted which forms a base from which they can explore their difference.

This raises the issue of personal boundaries and of choosing what is appropriate diversity for each of us, and to what extent we seek the anonymity of conformity or risk the glare and isolation of difference.

Individuals do choose and develop their own level of conformity, creating a culture they are comfortable with. This co-created conformity, the system influencing people and people influencing the system, is both comfortable and supportive. This could in part explain why new people would be expected to 'fit' and not disturb the comfort levels.

There is little doubt that a continuous high degree of conformity at work causes some people to lose sight of themselves and to identify themselves solely by title, grade, status, and so on. When people who do this are made redundant many of them feel that their very lives have been taken away from them and that they have nothing to live for. This degree of identity with one's job and the consequent loss of self is not healthy.

THE IMPORTANCE OF BOUNDARIES

It is a common practice for organizations to produce job descriptions aimed at defining what is needed of people. This is usually intended as a helpful device for bringing clarity to what people understand their roles to be. The modern approach is to specify these in term of the competencies needed. The result is to construct a bounded demand on the people which locks out many of their capabilities so that they are once again limited. Of course boundaries are an essential way for us to survive in the world. We all have to decide how revealing we want and need to be. This is a form of self-protection. It is also important that we respect other people's boundaries. Sexual harassment is clearly a failure to respect boundaries.

So boundaries both contain and limit us. We need them and yet we can allow them to limit us, especially if we just accept those placed on us by others. What we need is to find a balance between over- and under-exposure.

THE POWER OF DIVERSITY

The authors are coming to the belief that most organizations fear the power that they will release if they remove these limits and invite people to be themselves. If organizations can find the courage to embrace individual uniqueness, with all the jagged edges, then real high performance becomes possible. The process is not an easy one – it calls for an enlightened approach to management based on trust, freedom and responsibility.

Moving from a culture of sameness (including uniforms and dress codes) to a culture of diversity is a massive leap, probably one that is too great to be readily accepted by most organizations. However, it can be done if the following six principles are observed and the six necessary steps taken.

THE SIX PRINCIPLES FOR THE DIVERSE ORGANIZATION

The corporate vision embraces 'The desire to be different'

Balancing conformity and diversity with organizational aspirations and goals is never easy. As we saw in Chapters 4 and 9, organizational cultures carry the prejudices of the founders and the current management. These will expect people to conform with organization 'norms'. This can be very limiting unless it is balanced with 'the desire to be different'. By acknowledging the present culture and seeking to be different it is possible to find an appropriate balance between the two. The authors believe that 'the desire to be different' should be included as a mainstay of the corporate vision and mission.

Corporate leaders model diversity

When corporate leaders espouse one thing and do another the people they manage sense the incongruity and see such behaviour for what it is. For example, one chief executive insisted on all staff wearing the 'corporate wardrobe', but was never seen to wear it himself. For diversity to be fully seen and experienced within the organization the leaders of the organization have to lead by example, particularly in the way they appear, the way they behave both within and outside the organization and the way they interact with staff, customers, suppliers and the media.

Diversity is encouraged and rewarded

Being different should not be seen as 'breaking ranks' but as choosing to belong by being fully oneself. In this way people should be encouraged to be different and to make all aspects of themselves available to the organization. This does not mean encouraging people to be rebels, although this can sometimes be useful, but it does mean encouraging them to be unique and to stand up and stand out.

People are given 'freedom with responsibility'

Even contented slaves dream of freedom:

> Perfect freedom is reserved for the man
> who lives by his own work, and in that
> work does what he wants to do. (R.G. Collingwood)

We cannot have freedom without the responsibility of using it to the advantage of self and others. When we strive at the bidding of others we are not free in the sense of choosing what we do, nor are we responsible for our efforts. People work harder and better when they do it for themselves than they ever will when they do it for others. It is the exercise of choice and desire which signals freedom in the workplace.

Change is welcomed

Change is the very basis of existence and the natural process of the universe. Change is happening all the time. The apparent (illusory) idea we might have that things stay the same is due entirely to the simple fact that we use most of our energy resisting change and trying to keep things the same. Change is not something that we do or do not do. It is not something that we make happen, but we can influence the process of change.

We exist in the now, in this moment. What happens immediately becomes the past and we don't know what is going to happen next. When we try to look into the future we do so from where we are and by the time the future arrives we are somewhere else. This does not mean that planning is a waste of time. What it does mean is that we have to be ready to adapt our plans as things change and to welcome these changes.

Paradoxically, what we can do is accept that change is unmanageable. If we accept this then we have to change our focus to one of becoming more aware of the changes that are happening and their impact on our world. By doing this we can change our approach from one that seeks to chase and manage change to one that seeks to understand, welcome and react to change as it happens.

Corporate values will seek a balance between conformity and diversity

So here we face the dilemma. How do we create an environment where people can conform with a culture they have helped to create whilst at the same time being completely and uniquely themselves?

We believe that the answer lies in the way organizations espouse and foster values which include diversity. Such a value might be stated as follows:

> We value individual difference in all its manifestations whilst acknowledging the need for people to belong to and conform with a culture they have helped to create which embraces diversity.

These six principles for the diverse organization form the bedrock for the development of working practices which embrace diversity. If the principles are not fully established and observed in the behaviour of management there will be little hope of diversity existing to its fullest potential. However, when the principles are in place it is possible to take the steps necessary to build diversity into the corporate way of life.

THE SIX STEPS TO MAKING DIVERSITY HAPPEN

Create a vision which fully recognizes and embodies diversity

Vision and mission statements have come in for a lot of criticism, much of it well deserved. If a statement of a corporate vision is couched in terms which are clearly more of a PR exercise than a real attempt to state what the organization is about, then it deserves to be criticized.

What the authors believe is needed is a simple statement which embodies the organization's purpose and values. Such a statement might appear as follows:

> We exist to make a fair return on our shareholders' investment through the provision of efficient banking services to our customers whilst fully valuing their needs and those of our staff to be treated as independent and unique human beings.

Produce a 'Diversity Charter' containing the values and practices of diversity

The organization's 'Diversity Charter' would set out the specific details of how diversity will be built into the daily life of the organization. We propose that this

169

should appear as a simple guide rather than a high-minded-sounding document. It might well include the following sections:

- Recognition of individual difference (see Chapter 3).
- The exercise of choice (see Chapter 3).
- The freedom to develop individual potential (see Chapter 10).
- The exercise of responsibility.
- Statement of organizational boundaries (see Chapter 6).
- Recognition of personal boundaries (see Chapter 5).
- The human TOUCH (see Chapters 5 and 18).

Form diverse learning groups throughout the organization

One powerful way to capture the talent of people is by bringing them together to work in diverse learning groups. Diversity in this context means gathering people from different parts and levels of the organization. The aims of the groups could be to look at specified issues nominated by management or to create their own areas of interest. They would then work together harvesting the diverse creative talent of the members of the group to develop ideas and/or to focus on new initiatives being introduced by the organization.

Invite representatives from customers, investors and suppliers to join the learning groups

By opening up learning groups to other 'external' stakeholders a much wider forum for ideas and discussion would be created. This extension of diversity would, the authors believe, create a whole new meaning to the idea of cooperation and openness. Highly sensitive/confidential aspects of the organization could be held back from discussion at such groups, but outside such limited areas the scope for creativity could be enormous.

Build diversity into the performance management system

Performance management systems (Bentley 1996) need to fully reflect the organization's attitude towards diversity in that individual performance and development plans should incorporate the need for people to explore their full potential by bringing their unique mix of personality, skill and talent into the performance equation.

Provide guidance on best practice

One of the major problems with 'procedure guides', 'operating manuals' or whatever the written-down 'way to do things' is called is that they limit what people do and they cannot keep up with the speed of change as new ideas are incorporated into current 'best practice'. Instead of producing such 'bound' books, loose-leaf 'best practice guides' should be produced and changed as the need arises. These can be colour coded for different business processes and be created and circulated at different levels, for example for teams, divisions and/or companies.

CONCLUSION – DIVERSITY AT WORK

Diversity can be seen at work in those organizations where individuals are welcomed in the fullness of their individuality and where they are valued for the uniqueness of their contribution. In such organizations people belong *because* they are different, and it is their difference which is valued and rewarded. These are the organizations that do not try to smother their people with the blanket of a corporate identity, but where people contribute to the corporate identity by being fully themselves. Organizations where diversity is fully embraced are creative, exciting and innovative places to be. They bring out the best in their people, who in turn give of their best. The number of organizations where diversity is fully embraced is small but their numbers are growing. If you think your organization is one of these we want to hear from you; if not then we wish you success on your journey.

REFERENCE

Bentley, Trevor (1996), *Bridging the Performance Gap*, Aldershot: Gower.

Index